Wisdom and Worship

ROBERT DAVIDSON

Wisdom and Worship

*

The Edward Cadbury Lectures 1989

SCM PRESS
London

TRINITY PRESS INTERNATIONAL
Philadelphia

First published 1990

SCM Press Ltd
26–30 Tottenham Road
London N1 4BZ

Trinity Press International
3725 Chestnut Street
Philadelphia, Pa. 19104

British Library Cataloguing in Publication Data

Davidson, Robert
Wisdom and worship.
1. Christian doctrine. Faith
I. Title   II. Series
234.2

ISBN 0–334–02461–7

Library of Congress Cataloging-in-Publication Data

Davidson, Robert, M.A.
Wisdom and worship / Robert Davidson.
p.   cm.—(The Edward Cadbury lectures; 1989)
Includes bibliographical references
ISBN 0–334–02461–7; $12.95
1. Wisdom literature—History and criticism. 2. Public
worship—Biblical teaching. I. Title   II. Series.
BS1455.D38   1990
223'.06–dc20   90–39210

Typeset at The Spartan Press Ltd, Lymington, Hants
and printed in Great Britain by
Clays Ltd, St Ives plc

Contents

Preface

This book consists of the Edward Cadbury Lecture for 1988–89, delivered in the University of Birmingham in the Spring of 1989. I am grateful to Professor Frances Young and the trustees of the lectureship for the invitation to deliver the lectures, and to many members of the Department of Theology at Birmingham for the gracious welcome and hospitality extended to me while the lectures were being delivered. I owe a special debt to Rev. J. Ainslie McIntyre whose eagle eye rid the text of many infelicities, and who prepared the index.

I have decided to leave the lectures more or less in the form in which they were delivered, otherwise I might have found myself with another book, no doubt more closely argued and documented but almost certainly twice the length and perhaps still awaiting publication five years from now.

The lectures were an attempt to follow through more closely in one particular area – the relationship between worship and wisdom in ancient Israel – the general theme which was the basis of *The Courage to Doubt* (SCM Press 1983 and Trinity Press International 1989). The last lecture sought, however inadequately to try to root some of the issues raised in the worship of the Christian church today.

Introduction

The dialogue between faith and doubt has long fascinated me: not the confrontation which takes place between those who profess to believe in God and those who dismiss such belief as meaningless, but the dialogue which takes place within the experience of those who believe. There are, of course, definitions of faith and attitudes towards faith which firmly close the door on any kind of doubts. Such doubts are regarded as sinful, one of the many wiles of the devil. Thus a burden of guilt is often needlessly placed on those who find themselves forced through the harsh experiences of life to wrestle with questions to which they can find no easy answers and to live with doubts which honesty and integrity force upon them. Often this burden is reinforced by worship which ignores such doubts or invites God to forgive us for ever having entertained them. All of which is not only of little help to many people today, but is also, I believe, profoundly unbiblical.

In my earlier study, *The Courage to Doubt*, I tried to show that in Israel's experience there was an understanding of faith which left room for questioning, and which refused to sacrifice such radical questioning on the altar of religious conformity. This attitude towards faith is widely reflected in the various literary traditions in the Old Testament. It is reflected in the patriarchal narratives and in the definitive figure of Moses. It is part of prophetic experience and finds a natural home in the thinking of some of Israel's wisdom writers. It is an essential element in Israel's experience of worship, with the question 'Why?' being more frequently on the lips of the psalmists than 'Hallelujah'. Thus we find in ancient Israel an approach which sees doubt not as the opposite of faith but as an element in continuing and maturing faith, and the questioning of God not as a matter for guilt but as the expression of a faith which seeks to be more honestly grounded in experience.

The present study is an attempt to develop one aspect of this theme by looking more closely at the relationship between the wisdom thinkers in Israel and Israel's understanding of worship as that is reflected in the Psalms. It seeks to show that there is a two-way relationship. On the one hand there are the concerns of Israel's wisdom writers, concerns which they share with many of the sages in the wider world of the ancient Near East – the attempt to define the meaning of wisdom, the struggle to reconcile belief in a divine providence with a world riddled with injustice, their gazing across the ultimate frontier of death. Such things become part of Israel's worshipping experience and take on a new dimension in that context. On the other hand the insights which are central to worship – the reality, for example, of communion with God – are reflected in some at least of the wisdom writings; and where they are not reflected the search for wisdom faces an insoluble dilemma. The integration of wisdom and worship is seen at its clearest in the person of Jesus, son of Sirach, who is at one and the same time wisdom teacher and devout worshipper. A final chapter in this study seeks to explore some of the possible implications of taking seriously the relationship between wisdom and worship and the way in which worship can take on a new meaning for many people when they discover that they can bring the complexities of life today, its challenge and its questions, and share them with a worshipping community.

Chapter 1

What is Wisdom?

> But where can wisdom be found?
> And where is the source of understanding?

These two questions, with minor variation in language, occur twice, like a refrain, in the fascinating poem on wisdom in Job 28 (see verses 12 and 20). They give classic expression to problems which haunted the thinking of the wise men in Israel and in the wider world of the ancient Near East. On each occasion the questions are immediately answered. In spite of man's industrial ingenuity and skills, wisdom remains ultimately inaccessible to human discovery:

> No man knows the way to it;
> it is not found in the land of living men (v.13).

> No creature on earth can see it,
> and it is hidden from the birds of the air (v.21).

Interrogate the entire universe concerning this matchless treasure of wisdom – the Deep, the Sea, the Grave, Death itself – and the message comes echoing back, 'It is not in us' (v.14) or 'We know of it only by report' (v.22). From this agnostic judgment the poem turns to declare that from the beginning the source, the nature, the true depth of wisdom have been known only to God. It is, therefore, only in relationship with God that elusive wisdom can become part of human experience. Thus the poem ends with God saying to man:

> The fear of the Lord is wisdom,
> and to turn from evil is understanding (v.28).

The function of these concluding words and indeed their right
to any place in the poem have been vigorously discussed. Do they
represent a timid orthodox ending to the poem, 'a sort of nervous
corrective to the negative verdict on the human quest for wisdom
in the body of the poem'?[1] Is this theology attempting to dictate to
the restless, if frustrating, human search for wisdom celebrated
in the body of the poem, by insisting that there are certain 'no-go'
areas to which entry is restricted to those who can produce a pass
stamped by acceptable piety? This is an issue which affects not
only the relationship between the concluding words of Job 28 and
the rest of the poem, but also the relationship between Job 28 in
its entirety and the rest of the book of Job. The formal structure of
this chapter and its calm lyrical quality stand in sharp contrast to
what has preceded it. It has been variously regarded as 'an erratic
intrusion, an inspired intermezzo, a superfluous prelude, and an
orthodox afterthought'.[2] The view that would regard the poem as
extraneous to the rest of the book has, however, been increasingly called into question. It comes immediately after the
verbose, tense and somewhat bad-tempered dialogue between
Job and his three friends, a dialogue which raises in an acute form
issues which focus on the concept and claims of wisdom in
ancient Israel. It is therefore reasonable to assume that the
function of Job 28 may be to look back across the dialogue, to
comment upon its adequacy or inadequacy, and perhaps at the
same time to act as the prelude to the rest of the book which
climaxes in the speeches on divine wisdom in chapters 38–41.[3]
Once we look at Job 28 in this light, particularly with reference to
the preceding dialogue, several important issues germane to the
nature and limitations of wisdom in ancient Israel arise.

1. The concluding verse of Job 28 echoes the initial description
of Job in the prologue as a man who 'feared God and turned from
evil' (1.1). According to the wisdom teaching preserved in the
book of Proverbs there is a paradoxical relationship between such
'fear of the Lord and turning from evil' and wisdom and
understanding. On the one hand it is wisdom and understanding
that lead the way to the fear of the Lord and the blameless life:

> My son, if you take my words to heart
> and lay up my commands in your mind,
> giving your attention to wisdom

and your mind to discernment,
if you summon understanding to your aid
and invoke discernment,
if you seek her out like silver
and dig for her like buried treasure,
then you will understand the fear of the Lord
and attain to the knowledge of God;
for the Lord bestows wisdom
and teaches knowledge and understanding.
Out of his store he endows the upright with ability
as a shield for those who live blameless lives;
for he guards the course of justice
and keeps watch over the way of his loyal servants
(Prov.2.1–8).

On this view the 'fear of the Lord' is the end product of a prior commitment to wisdom. On the other hand the fear of the Lord is elsewhere claimed to be the beginning of or 'the first step' to wisdom (Prov.9.10), the beginning or foundation of knowledge (Prov.1.7); a view echoed by a Psalmist:

The fear of the Lord is the beginning of wisdom,
and they who live by it grow in understanding.
Praise will be his for ever (Ps.111.10).

This paradoxical relationship has been the subject of considerable discussion in the analysis of Israel's wisdom traditions. Was there, as has been claimed, an early secular tradition of wisdom in Israel, or at least a wisdom tradition which existed independently of Israel's mainstream religious traditions, and which was perhaps never fully integrated into them? Are therefore the passages which link the fear of the Lord with wisdom, either as its source or end product, nothing more than late attempts to reconcile what is perhaps irreconcilable, the product of post-exilic piety. This view has been well expressed by Blenkinsopp:

The evidence for adaptation and development within the book (i.e. Proverbs) leads to the conclusion that collections of proverbs expressing the common ethos of the scribal schools have been modified and supplemented by religious teachers after the Babylonian exile. Characteristic of the latter is the fear of Yahweh as epitome of the moral life (e.g. 10:27), the belief in

Yahweh as the sustainer of the moral order (e.g. 10:3), the description of certain types of conduct as 'an abomination to Yahweh' (e.g. 11:1,20 . . . .), the use of specific religious categories like sin, prayer and sacrifice, and the contrast, monotonously repeated, between the fate of the righteous and the wicked.[4]

Is therefore wisdom in early Israel, and in the wider world of the ancient Near East, to be thought of as essentially pragmatic as opposed to pietistic, the product of those who by shrewd observation of human life in all its rich variety, and by rational analysis of human experience, operated independently of any concept of revelation? We shall have occasion to return to this question later.

2. With its stress upon the inaccessability of wisdom, wisdom beyond human discovery and analysis, Job 28 may be taken as legitimate critical comment upon the attitudes adopted both by Job's friends and by Job himself in the preceding dialogue. Their attempts to retain faith in a God worthy of respect, in face of a world riddled by apparently inexplicable suffering and tragedy, raise as many questions as they answer.

(*a*) As far as the friends are concerned, Eliphaz, who plays the lead role, seeks to respond to Job's initial outburst of agonized 'whys' –

Why was I not still-born,
why did I not die when I came out of my mother's womb?
(3.11 cf.12)

Why should the sufferer be born to see the light?
Why is life given to men who find it so bitter? (3.20)

Why should a man be born to wander blindly,
hedged in by God on every side? (3.23)

He argues – and claims the authority of revelation for so doing – that there are recognizable boundaries to human knowledge. We are not God, nor any kind of supernatural species. We are mortals with a fleeting hold on life, sinners with a limited perspective (see chapter 4). Moreover there is, he argues, a type of human wisdom, arrogant human wisdom, which is no more than a form of self-destructive cleverness. There is, however, one issue upon which Eliphaz will not compromise; and here he reflects the adamant view of all the friends. There exists, he asserts, a fixed divinely-given order built into life. To live in accordance with this order is the mark of the truly wise man, not least when it involves accepting 'the discipline of God' (5.17). Such a life brings with it its own tangible rewards, success and security, numerous descendants and longevity (cf. Prov.3.1–4; 4.7–9). To depart from or to challenge this order is the mark of the fool or the wicked and brings inevitable disaster. This he spells out initially in a passage in 5.17ff. which has many of the characteristic features of wisdom literature: the 'happiness' formula, 'Happy the man whom God rebukes' (5.17); the ascending numerical saying,

> You may meet disaster six times, and he will save you;
> seven times, and no harm shall touch you (5.19).

Moreover he backs up what he has to say by appealing to experience:

> We have inquired into all this, and so it is;
> this we have heard, and you may know it for the truth
> (5.27).

When Job later stubbornly and aggressively refuses to accept that this makes sense of his own experience, Eliphaz accuses him of parting company from the wise in Israel:

> Would a wise man give vent to such foolish notions
> and answer with a bellyful of wind?
>
> Were you born first of mankind?
> Were you brought forth before the hills?
> Do you listen in God's secret council
> or usurp all wisdom for yourself alone?
> What do you know that we do not know?
> What insight have you that we do not share?
> We have age and white hairs in our company,
> men older than your father (15.2,7–10).

Job, he asserts, has thrown down the gauntlet to:

> What has been handed down by wise men
> and was not concealed from them by their fathers (15.18).

So confident is Eliphaz of this that he ends up rewriting Job's life to fit in with this wisdom script (22.5–11), a not uncommon response of the inflexible religious mind under pressure. If the facts won't fit in with assumptions, so much the worse for the facts. Zophar is equally uncompromising. In face of Job's protestations that he is innocent of any evil that could possibly justify the enormity of his suffering, Zophar retorts:

> Are you to talk nonsense and no one rebuke you?
> You claim that your opinions are sound;
> you say to God, 'I am spotless in your sight'.
> But if only God would speak
> and open his lips to talk with you,
> and expound to you the secrets of wisdom,
> for how wonderful are its effects! (11.3–6)

He goes on to underline the limits of human understanding; he draws attention to 'the mystery of God', the 'perfection of the Almighty', totally beyond our grasp (11.7). It is evident, however, that Job's plight does not come into this category of mystery; it does not lie beyond the frontiers of human understanding:

> If only you had directed your heart rightly
> and spread out your hands to pray to him!
> If you have wrongdoing in hand, thrust it away;
> let no iniquity make its home with you (11.13–14).

The poem in Job 28 seems to be challenging this assumption. The slick and easy answers to the problem of suffering which the friends are pedalling, no matter how strong the appeal they make to traditional views, are in effect no answers, at best pseudo-wisdom. The claim to human wisdom needs to be further circumscribed than the friends are prepared to admit, the mystery is greater than they recognize.

(*b*) What of Job himself? He has all the marks of one of the wise men in the ancient world. The arguments of the friends fail to impress him precisely because they fall foul of his own bitter experience of life. Zophar, in whose eyes Job's stubborn rebelliousness betokens a man bereft of wisdom, calls for a radical change of heart by Job and at the same time indicates his scepticism as to whether it is possible by quoting what may well be a proverbial saying:

> Can a fool grow wise?
> can a wild ass's foal be born a man? (11.12)

To this Job retorts:

> No doubt you are perfect men
> and absolute wisdom is yours!
> But I have sense as well as you;
> in nothing do I fall short of you;
> what gifts indeed have you that
> others have not? (12.2–3)

He accepts that true wisdom is one of the characteristics of God:

> Wisdom and might are his,
> with him are firmness and understanding (12.13):

yet he is determined to present his case before this divine judge, in the confidence that the arguments of his friends do not, and cannot, represent true wisdom:

> But you, you fabricate lies. You are all quacks.
> If only you would remain silent,
> It would count as wisdom for you
> > (13.5cf.26.3 – Habel's translation).

In the light of Proverbs 17.28 this comment may well imply that Job considers his friends to be no better than fools:

> Even a fool, if he holds his peace, is thought wise;
> keep your mouth shut and show your good sense.

While the friends never doubt that Job must be brought to see the folly of what they can only regard as his blasphemous and heretical views, Job insists that the boot is really on the other foot:

> But as for all of you, turn back! Come on now!
> I do not find a wise person among you (17.10 – Habel).

Yet this uncompromising dismissal of the arguments of the friends and the wisdom tradition they represent, allied to Job's passionate belief that if only he could present his case to God he would be bound to be acquitted (13.3ff.), point to a man who may himself be in danger of stepping beyond the frontiers of human wisdom. Job may rightly object to the straight-jacket of retribution within which the others have imprisoned God, but is he not himself in danger of locking God into his own questions and insisting that God come up with answers acceptable to him? In this context Job 28 may be arguing that it is one thing to search for answers and to be dissatisfied with the answers others give, it is another thing to believe that God can be forced into giving the answers you want, or indeed that God exists solely to provide such answers.

In terms, therefore, of the attitudes of both Job and his friends chapter 28 of the book of Job may be raising legitimate questions about human claims to wisdom. There is, however, another respect in which the chapter remains profoundly unhelpful. If the final verse echoes, as we have seen, the initial description of Job as a man 'who feared God and turned from evil' (1.1), may we not respond by saying 'here we go again; back to where we started'. The poem has obviously nothing to say except to remind us

> The fear of the Lord is wisdom,
> and to turn from evil is understanding.

Job has been introduced to us as a man who had such wisdom and understanding, yet this wisdom and understanding clearly do not help him to come to terms with his suffering and the questions which it raises in his mind. Does this mean then that in Israel, wisdom, even when given a theological orientation, is fatally flawed; and if so how does it interact at this point with other aspects of Israel's religious traditions? It is this interaction, particularly with Israel's tradition of worship as reflected in the Psalms, which we wish to explore further.

But what is wisdom? If Job 28 raises the question 'where can wisdom be found?', modern scholarship is not even sure what it is looking for in terms of ancient Israelite wisdom. It has been rightly said '. . . at present there are several different notions about the historical and theological development, no one definition of wisdom capable of winning consensus, much disagreement about the social setting and class of wisdom, and a lack of uniformity about the nature and development of some fundamental literary forms in the wisdom tradition.'[5] This need hardly surprise us since we are dealing with concepts and with a literary tradition which long pre-dates the existence of Israel in the ancient Near East, which early found a natural home in Israel, probably in family and clan life, and which at the end of the Old Testament period were providing Judaism with a powerful theological symbol and an enticing bridge into the world of Hellenistic thought and culture. The very nature of the Old Testament, not least its theological selectivity, means that every attempt to provide a historical description of such a long-lasting phenomenon in ancient Israel must be tentative. There was, however, until comparatively recently a widely held assumption that from the religious and theological perspective wisdom, as represented by a book such as Proverbs, was of only marginal significance, certainly until the post-exilic period. Wisdom was the Cinderella in the household of Israel's faith. There were those who argued that, looked at from the standpoint of mainstream Yahwistic faith, the wisdom tradition was essentially secular. Cinderella's lowly role was assigned to her by a wicked stepmother, Dame Old Testament Theology, and her ugly sisters went serenely to the ball in carriages marked 'Covenant' – the peculiar, historically grounded relationship between Yahweh and Israel – or 'Salvation History', that indissoluble blend of event and interpretation which was the distinctive hallmark of Israel's understanding of revelation. Not even all the charms of 'the fear of the Lord', invoked by an eleventh hour fairy godmother, could redeem this Cinderella. As John Bright put it '. . . some parts of the Old Testament are far less clearly expressive of Israel's distinctive understanding of reality than others, some parts (and one thinks of such a book as Proverbs) seem to be only peripherally related to it, while others (for example Ecclesiastes) even question some of its essential features.'[6] Bright does not deny that Israel's distinctive relationship to God lies assumed in the background to such books, but in themselves they have no positive contribution to make to Israel's theology. The more the 'distinctive' or what was thought to be 'unique' in Israel's experience became the norm for Old Testament theology, the less chance wisdom had of being taken seriously, since it was difficult to deny that there were close affinities in content and form between wisdom material within the Old Testament and wisdom material from the wider world of the ancient Near East, particularly from Mesopotamian and Egyptian sources.[7]

The scene has now dramatically changed. The wicked step-mother has gone through a period of self doubt and is still in the throes of an identity crisis. The dictates of the ugly sisters no longer rule unchallenged; and like many another person marginalized or despised by society, wisdom Cinderella has lived to take her revenge. Indeed she has become positively aggressive in flaunting her charms. Few areas of Israel's thought or literature have emerged unscathed from her blandishments. The influence of wisdom has been traced in much narrative material in the Old Testament, for example in the creation stories in Genesis 2–3 and in the Joseph story in Genesis 37ff. What has often been regarded as one of the earliest narratives in the Old Testament, the so-called succession narrative in II Sam.9–20 and I Kings 1–2, has been viewed as a dramatization of proverbial wisdom, an attempt 'to teach the doctrines of the wisdom schools':[8] while at the other end of the Old Testament time span the book of Esther has been read as an 'historicized wisdom tale'.[9] The book of Deuteronomy has been traced to political thinkers who flourished under the Hebrew monarchy and who shared some of the major concerns of the wisdom tradition, particularly the emphasis upon humanism and retribution.[10] From Amos to Second Isaiah within the prophetic corpus, wisdom themes, wisdom language, wisdom literary forms have been found. The thesis has been propounded, notably on the basis of Daniel 1–6, that it is wisdom rather than prophecy which provided the matrix out of which Apocalyptic sprang.[11]

Not all such claims for wisdom influence are well founded. But one thing is clear. The sharp distinctions which were once drawn between different strands in Israel's traditions must be treated with considerable caution. To regard the prophets, for example, as being antithetic to, or inhabiting a wholly different thought world from that of the wisdom teachers will not do. In particular the theological neutrality or indifference of wisdom must be seriously questioned. It has been noted that creation theology has been widely used in the wisdom literature to deal with basic human problems, not least that of suffering, or to defend God's presence and justice in a world which often seems to deny both.[12] The burden of proof must lie with those who wish to argue that there was in Israel, or in the wider world of the ancient Near East, a wisdom tradition which may be labelled 'secular' rather than religious. Of course it is possible to define the concerns of the wise in language which does not seem to employ specifically theological concepts – the search for an understanding of order within nature and society, the striving for meaning and self-understanding, the attempt so to regulate daily life in the light of such order and meaning that people would know how to act, mid the choices and the perplexing circumstances of life, in such a way that success could be guaranteed and failure avoided. But behind the search lay a fundamental religious premise. The order within nature and society was divinely given, part of the cosmos as it had been determined by the gods 'in the beginning'; and that order which the wise sought to explore and comprehend was the same order which the community was concerned to acknowledge, to respond to and to maintain in its various cultic practices and religious festivals.

When this concept of order was under threat, for example by war, civil disturbance or natural catastrophe, the wise could give voice to serious questioning and indeed at times to total perplexity if not cynicism – witness, from the First Intermediate Period in Egypt (twenty-second and twenty-first centuries BCE) the 'Dialogue of a man with his Ba' and 'The Harper's Song', and from Mesopotamia 'The Babylonian Theodicy' and the 'Dialogue of Pessimism'.[13] In the end, however, there was no alternative to holding on to some understanding of a divine order which might defy rational human understanding, but must still exist somehow and somewhere. Thus in the so-called 'Babylonian Theodicy', an acrostic poem of twenty-seven stanzas of argument between a 'righteous sufferer' and 'a friend', the sufferer ends up not in an attitude of Promethean defiance of the gods, but as a suppliant who prays for the return of his protecting deities, and hopes against hope that there will come a time when Shamash, the god of justice, will recognize that this suppliant is truly pious and will reward him accordingly.[14] A document for the New Kingdom in Egypt (sixteenth century BCE onwards) 'In Praise of Learned Scribes'[15] sharply criticizes certain elements in contemporary religious practice, particularly the lavish mortuary cults; it argues that the scribes have a more lasting claim to fame than crumbling tombs, 'though they are gone and their names are forgotten, it is writing that makes them remembered'. The same scribes, however, though at times they may indulge in bitter sarcasm and may end up like Ecclesiastes saying, 'follow your desire as long as you live . . . until there comes for you that day of mourning' (The Harper's Song), nevertheless repeatedly call for the restoration of order by the gods and by men, an order within which inner tranquillity and social welfare may again be found. There is no justification for taking the most critical and cynical comments from the wise in Mesopotamia, Egypt or Israel, ignoring their cultural context, and interpreting them in the light of modern secularist assumptions. As L. G. Perdue in *Wisdom and Cult* has rightly claimed, it is wide of the mark to view the wise in Israel, or elsewhere in the ancient Near East, as 'internationalist' cosmopolitan humanists and secularists who functioned with empirical and rational epistemologies, were indifferent to the sphere of the cult, and its demand for confrontation and participation, were often disdainful of cultic observance and participants, and negatively criticized matters of cult.[16]

In Israel we should view the attitude of the wise, not as non-theological over against a religious tradition dominated by a view of a God who revealed himself in historical events, but rather as an alternative and equally valid way of doing theology. The Old Testament as a whole, within the framework of belief in Yahweh's presence, purposes and activity in the world, invites us to share in a theological pluralism. In the context of such pluralism the wisdom tradition has its own distinctive contribution to make. Different ways of doing theology, a different theological vocabulary may lie side by side within the one book in the Old Testament. The book of Genesis is an interesting case study in this respect. In the stories of the patriarchs, Abraham, Isaac and Jacob in chapters 12–33, there is a clearly defined theological style and vocabulary. It lays heavy emphasis upon God's initiative and God's speech:

The Lord said to Abram, 'Leave your own country . . .' (12.1).

The Lord said to Abram, 'Raise your eyes and look into the distance from the place where you are, north and south, east and west . . .' (13.14).

After this the word of the Lord came to Abram in a vision. He said, 'Do not be afraid, Abram, I am giving you a great reward . . .' (15.1; cf. 15.7, 13, 18; 17.1,15; 18.10,13).

The Lord appeared to Isaac and said to him, 'Do not go down to Egypt' (26.2; cf.v.24).

The Lord . . . said (to Jacob), 'I am the Lord, the God of your father Abraham and the God of Isaac' (28.13).

The Lord said to Rebecca, 'Two nations in your womb, two peoples going their own way from birth' (25.23).

Similarly these narratives contain a series of theophanies, often associated with age-old cultic centres:

The Lord appeared to Abraham by the terebinths of Mamre (18.1).

Isaac went up country from there to Beersheba. That same night the Lord appeared to him there . . . (26.23).

Jacob experiences his theophany in his dream at Bethel (28.11–19), and has his mysterious encounter at the brook Jabbok (32.22–32; cf.46.2).

When, however, we turn to the Joseph story in Genesis 37ff., a story which has strong affinities with wisdom material, we enter a different theological world. At no point does the narrative claim that God spoke directly to Joseph. Joseph may have dreams (37.5–11), which intensify his brothers' jealousy and thus set in motion subsequent events, but it is not claimed that God spoke to Joseph in these dreams. Pharaoh has dreams, through which Joseph claims that God is showing to Pharaoh what is going to happen, but at least the meaning of what God intends is not clear to Pharaoh, and Joseph in his interpretation of the dreams uses techniques of dream interpretation well known and widely practised in ancient Egypt. Nor are there any theophanies. Yet the narrative is profoundly theological. In Joseph's life through family jealousy and enslavement in Egypt, from prison to the Ministry of Agriculture and the headship of the Egyptian civil service, there runs the outworking of God's purposes, purposes unknown to the participants at the time, but nonetheless certain in the eyes of the narrator. Joseph in several far from promising situations makes good because the Lord was with him (39.2,23), and when he finally reveals his identity to his anxious brothers, he says: Do not be disturbed or angry with yourselves because you sold me here: for God sent me before you to preserve life . . .

So it was not you who sent me here but God (45.5,8); sentiments
which he reassuringly repeats to the brothers after the death of
their father, . . . Fear not, for am I in the place of God? As for you,
you meant evil against me, but God meant it for good, to bring it
about that many people should be kept alive, as they are today
(50.20). There is here belief in providence, in a

> . . . divinity that shapes our ends,
> rough-hew them how we will (*Hamlet* ii.10),

and that divinity is none other than Yahweh the God of Israel.
What the Joseph story illustrates is an alternative way of speaking
and thinking theologically from that found in the earlier chapters
of Genesis.

There is every reason to believe that such theological pluralism
is not merely the product of the final editing of texts – though that
may have contributed to it – but the reflection of a long and
complex process within the experience of Israel. It is worth,
therefore, attempting to tease out the relationship, if any,
between the typically wisdom way of speaking and thinking with
its theological premises, and Israel's experience of worship,
particularly as that is reflected in the Psalms.

Chapter 2

Defining the Wisdom Element
in the Psalms

When the question of the relationship between the wisdom tradition in the Old Testament and worship in Israel is raised, it usually centres upon and is discussed in terms of the extent to which there is a clearly definable category of Psalms to which we can give the title 'Wisdom Psalms'. One of the weaknesses in this approach, however, lies in the fact that there is very little agreement as to what constitutes a Wisdom Psalm. It was H. Gunkel in 1926 who first identified within the Psalter a genre which he called *Weisheitsdichtung*, and to it he assigned eight Psalms (1, 37, 49, 73, 112, 127, 128 and 133), although he admitted that there were other Psalms showing evidence of wisdom influence. The criteria for such a classification were, and have remained, twofold:

1. the presence of wisdom language and wisdom rhetorical devices, such as the alphabetic acrostic pattern, numerical sayings, the address of the teacher to his 'sons', and the *'ashre'* (happy the person who) statement.

2. the presence of themes characteristic of the wisdom writings, for example the sharp contrast between the righteous and the wicked, the reality of retribution.

Using such criteria Gunkel's eight Wisdom Psalms have by others been expanded to fifteen or contracted to three. Nor have there been lacking voices who have questioned whether such a category is useful or necessary, and have argued that all the so-called 'Wisdom Psalms' may easily be incorporated into other more clearly defined Psalm categories. All of which means that there is a certain lack of precision in the criteria being used, however useful the criteria may be.

There is, moreover, no firm agreement as to the date or the sociological context of such Psalms. Although it has been argued that the wise in Israel, as elsewhere in the ancient Near East, had a lively interest in the cult from an early period, and may have contributed material for cultic use in any period,[1] there has been a widespread assumption that most, if not all, of the Wisdom Psalms are to be dated to the post-exilic period, and reflect a disintegration of earlier psalm categories. Thus Mowinckel regarded them as 'late didactic poems'.[2] Janzen, although viewing such psalms as the work of sages operating in the context of wisdom schools located near the temple, and as being designed initially for a two-fold purpose, cultic devotion and wisdom instruction, nevertheless argues that in their present literary form, the Wisdom Psalms are intended primarily for purposes of instruction, not for the cult, and assigns them to the intertestamental period, positing instruction in the synagogue as their natural setting.[3] A more recent study by J. H. Kuntz tries to keep open both cultic use for the community of faith gathered for worship either in temple or later synagogue, and non-cultic use in home, street, city gate and court. He is wisely cautious about dating, arguing that it is doubtful whether at any time in the life of ancient Israel instruction and praise were lacking within the family setting.[4]

When the definition, the number, the date and the sociological setting of the Wisdom Psalms admit of such diverse interpretations, it is tempting to suggest that a somewhat different approach to the question of the relationship between the wisdom traditions and the Psalms is needed. Roland E. Murphy is surely right in arguing that the relationship between the wisdom literature and other Old Testament traditions cannot be settled purely on linguistic grounds but needs to be reformulated in terms of a *shared approach to reality*. 'It is not a question of the direct influence of the sage or of the wisdom literature, but rather of an approach to reality which was shared by all Israelites in varying degrees.' Although the wise were the experts whose teaching was crystallized in a body of wisdom literature, 'the mentality itself was much broader than the literary remains that have come down to us'.[5] Such a shared approach to reality can be consistent with different ways of doing theology. It follows that the place or the influence of wisdom in the Psalms and in the life of the community gathered for worship cannot be settled solely on the basis of classifying certain Psalms on form-critical grounds as Wisdom Psalms. The net must be spread more widely; but how widely?

Let us begin by considering the thesis contained in L. G. Perdue's book, *Wisdom and Cult* (1977).[6] A detailed analysis of wisdom material from the ancient Near East, Mesopotamia and Egypt as well as Israel, leads Perdue to the conclusion that, 'the traditional wise regarded the cult to be an important compartment within the orders of reality, and therefore merited sapiential scrutiny and demanded sagacious participation',[7] i.e. the wise, while not uncritical of the cult, recognized the important role which worship played in the life of the community and were prepared to make their own contribution to it. When it comes to assessing what that contribution is, two strands need to be recognized. Along one line wisdom and worship become fully integrated, certainly by the second century BCE in the Wisdom of Ben Sirach in whom, to quote G. von Rad 'the teacher becomes the worshipper'. With his identification of wisdom with torah, with his interest in Israel's historical traditions, with his recurring prayers, Ben Sirach 'regards cultic religion as an essential and important part of Israel's religious heritage and the wise man's own religious devotion.'[8] Along another line, however, there are wisdom teachers, notably Job and Ecclesiastes, who raise serious questions about the very theological foundations of Israel's worship. How do the Wisdom Psalms fit into this picture? Here Perdue raises the question as to whether such Psalms were written for use in the cult or whether they were didactic poems, academic exercises designed to instruct students seeking enlightenment from the sages. Surveying the Psalms which are normally classified as Wisdom Psalms he argues that Psalms 1, 37, 49 and 112, which show no evidence of cultic terminology and conform to no recognized cultic norms, should be regarded solely as didactic poems intended for instructional purposes, e.g., to stimulate discussion on the problem of theodicy, and to do so in the context of a wisdom school, or in the case of Psalm 49 perhaps in the milieu of court circles since the wealthy and the 'men of the world' are part of its audience. Psalms 32, 34 and 73, while containing cultic material, were nevertheless not written for use in the cult. Psalm 34, for example, contains in verses 2–11 a psalm of individual thanksgiving, but this 'has been taken by a wisdom teacher and used as a model thanksgiving for the instruction of young schoolboys in the "fear of the Lord".'[9] Only Psalms 19A, 19B and 119 were composed by the wise 'with an eye on their being used in the sacred liturgies'.[10]

Much of this is more ingenious than convincing. It assumes far more than we have any right to assume about the teaching techniques of the wise, the circles within which they operated in Ancient Israel, and their educational methods. It does nothing to explain why it is that certain didactic poems, originally without any cultic reference or interest, take their place in a collection of Psalms central to Israel's worship. While Perdue at this point follows the common explanation of Psalm 1 as having been placed in its present position as an introduction to the Psalter by a scribal redactor, this can hardly account for the present position of Psalms 37, 49 and 112. There is, however, a more fundamental issue at stake here. Perdue works throughout with the assumption that such didactic poems or Wisdom Psalms contain material which enables us to assess the attitude of the wise towards the cult in Israel: it is equally possible, and just as likely, that we should approach the issue from the other end. Instead of didactic poems, designed for the instruction of schoolboys, poems which have somehow or other found their place in Israel's hymn book, is it not more reasonable to assume that we are dealing with material which had its original home in wisdom circles, but which has been consciously taken, adapted and integrated into the community's worship by those responsible for directing such worship or influencing it.

There are broadly two ways in which this could have happened:

1. Those responsible for Israel's worship deliberately used wisdom material because they had a shared approach to reality with wisdom teachers and believed that such teaching contributed insights or raised crucial questions which ought to be central to Israel's experience of worship. Furthermore, they did this believing that such insights and questions could be seen in a new light when set in the context of worship. Let me try to

illustrate by the example of the Scottish Paraphrases of 1781 which take passages of scripture and adapt them for use in congregational worship.[11] Consider the paraphrase of Isaiah 40.27ff. In the King James Version, from which the paraphrase was made, verse 27 reads as follows: 'Why sayest thou, O Jacob, and speakest, O Israel, My way is hid from the Lord, and my judgment is passed over from my God?' This is rendered:

> Why pourest thou forth thine anxious plaint
>   despairing of relief,
> As if the Lord o'erlooked thy cause,
>   and did not heed thy grief.

Note how the paraphrase seeks to make the verse more accessible and more personal to the worshipper both by its omission of the references to Jacob and Israel, thus leaving the worshipper free to identify himself or herself with the text; and by transposing the rather formal language of 'My way' and 'my judgment' into

> As if the Lord o'erlooked thy cause,
>   and did not heed thy grief.

Verse 28 is rendered in the King James Version 'Hast thou not known? hast thou not heard, that the everlasting God, the Lord the Creator of the ends of the earth, fainteth not, neither is weary? there is no searching of his understanding.' These magnificent words are expanded into three verses, with 28b becoming

> Art thou afraid his power shall fail
> When comes thy evil day?
> And can an all-creating arm
> Grow weary or decay?

> Supreme in wisdom as in power
> The Rock of ages stands;
> Though him thou canst not see, nor trace
> The working of his hands.

The concluding words giving a more personal and pious misinterpretation of the original 'there is no searching of his understanding', encouraging the worshipper to believe when he cannot see.

The vivid imagery of the concluding words of the chapter: 'they shall mount up with wings as eagles; they shall run, and not be weary; and they shall walk, and not faint' becomes through a process of expansion and spiritualization:

> They with unwearied feet shall tread
> The path of life divine;
> With growing ardour onward move,
> With growing brightness shine.
>
> On eagles' wings they mount, they soar,
> Their wings are faith and love,
> Till, past the cloudy regions here,
> They rise to heaven above.

These concluding words owe more to later Christian piety than to what is conveyed by the original text.

Such a paraphrase provides an interesting example of the way in which people who were concerned to enrich the worship of the community take passages from scripture, put them into metrical form – the merits of which are perhaps best left undiscussed – and adapt them to speak more directly to those who gather for worship, while believing, rightly or wrongly, that they are leaving the basic theological thrust of the passage unchanged. I do not wish to push this analogy too far. It is separated from the Psalms by centuries of Jewish and Christian tradition and by the existence of a canon of sacred scripture; but if those who were responsible for shaping Israel's worship had 'a shared approach to reality' with some of the wisdom teachers and were familiar with their work, either in oral or written form, could they not have done something similar in terms of the important theological issues which these teachers were raising? The very act of transferring such teaching into this new context of worship, however, means that it will be approached in a new light and with a new set of assumptions. If, for example, we find in the wisdom writings a doctrine of retribution and an exploration of the limits within such a doctrine is valid (cf. Job and Ecclesiastes), and there are Psalms which handle the same issues '. . . it seems plausible to assume that the wisdom sayings in these Psalms intend to do more than teach: they need to comfort, to protest, to assure, to affirm the presence of God's loving kindness. In doing so the didactic nature of the individual element is transformed through the cultic corporate medium.'[12] The highly cerebral nature of much of the wisdom material will become more closely a matter of the heart.

2. There is, however, another possibility that we ought to keep in mind. It may be true, as von Rad claims, that it is only when we come to Ben Sirach in the second century BCE that there is incontrovertible evidence that 'the teacher becomes the worshipper' but in view of the long established links which exist between wisdom teachers and the cult (cf.Perdue), it is not unlikely that some of the Wisdom Psalms may be evidence for the teacher as worshipper at an earlier date. If in face of some of the challenging and uncomfortable realities there comes to the wise an ever increasing conviction that Wisdom ultimately lies beyond human comprehension or discovery, and that, at the heart of life and the universe, there is a Wisdom which transcends definition and is known only to God, then what more natural than that a wisdom teacher should himself take some of the issues he explores, particularly those which push him to the frontiers of human understanding, and seek to look at them anew in the context of worship and the community's religious heritage which is being celebrated and relived in worship. A wisdom teacher, like a priest, a prophet or the king, like many another ordinary person, could also be a worshipper, bringing his own particular concerns with him to worship. Von Rad's argument is based upon a datable document which clearly and skilfully blends wisdom material with Israel's religious heritage as expressed in worship. If, however, we find the same blend in certain of the Psalms why should this not be evidence for the teacher as worshipper at an earlier period, even though we may have to be less than certain as to precisely when? The following words have been applied to the author of Psalm 73. 'The psalmist solved his problems *both* by visiting the temple *and* by participating in the discussions of the nearby wisdom schools.'[13] These words are capable of wider application.

Either of the above approaches, or both, may reasonably account for the presence of wisdom material, rhetorical characteristics and themes, within the Psalms, both within the Psalms usually classified as Wisdom Psalms and much more widely. Let us now try to illustrate both the presence of wisdom character-

istics and themes and the subtle way in which they are recast in the
Psalms by looking at one of the literary features found both in
wisdom material and in the Psalms. One of the literary or rhetorical
features of wisdom teaching is the so-called *'ashre'* sayings. The
'ashre' sayings have indeed been regarded by J. H. Kuntz as the
most important of the seven rhetorical criteria characteristic of the
Wisdom Psalms.[14] The Hebrew word *'ashre'* has traditionally been
rendered 'blessed' – thus the King James Version with occasional
lapses into 'happy'; particularly when the passage refers to what
may be regarded as mundane blessings, such as filled barns,
healthy livestock, or a quiverful of children (Ps. 127.5); or with
reference to conduct which may raise certain religious eyebrows,
such as the ending to Psalm 137 which it renders: 'O daughter of
Babylon, who art to be destroyed; happy shall he be, that
rewardeth thee as thou hast served us. Happy shall he be that
taketh and dasheth thy little ones against the stones.' Presumably
it was thought that in such a case you could be 'happy' without
being 'blessed' in a more deeply religious sense, a distinction
which the NIV retains by rendering *'ashre'* 'blessed', except in
Psalm 137. The RSV similarly tends to render 'blessed' though it
spreads the 'happy' rendering more widely. Both NEB and GNB
opt for 'happy' throughout. It has been suggested that *'ashre'*
ought to be translated 'to be envied', 'to be congratulated'. It might
equally be claimed, more colloquially, that it is a description of
someone who is 'on the ball' as far as his attitude to and his
response to life are concerned. Although there are one or two
examples of *'ashre'* sayings scattered elsewhere in the Old
Testament, in narrative and in prophetic passages,[15] they occur
predominantly in the wisdom literature in Proverbs, Job and
Ecclesiastes, and most frequently of all in the Psalms.

In the wisdom literature the link is sometimes specifically made
with wisdom (*hokma*), and its synonyms. Thus:

> Happy is the man who finds wisdom,
> and the man who gets understanding (Prov. 3.13).

These words introduce a section which goes on to describe
wisdom as being

> . . . a tree of life to those who lay hold on her;
> those who hold her fast are called happy (Prov. 3.18).

with the concluding words 'are called happy' being a translation of a verbal form from the same Hebrew root as *'ashre'*. In Proverbs 8 Dame Wisdom concludes her address to the sons of men in the following terms:

> And now, my sons, listen to me:
> happy are those who keep my ways.
> Hear instruction and be wise,
> and do not neglect it (Prov. 8.32–33).

What is on offer to those who heed Dame Wisdom's advice is described as 'life' in contract to 'death', and obtaining the favour of the Lord (v.35).

The same link with wisdom is stressed in the narrative occurrence in I Kings 10.8 (II Chron. 9.7) where the Queen of Sheba panders to Solomon's ego by saying: 'Happy are your wives! Happy are your servants who continually stand before you and hear your wisdom.'

Elsewhere in the wisdom literature such *'ashre'* sayings point to desirable conduct in the context of an antithetical proverb:

> He who despises his neighbour (or with the LXX 'a
>   hungry man') does wrong,
> but he who is generous to the poor is happy (Prov. 14.21).

or describe the ideal social order, seen through the eyes of a benevolent or blinkered aristocracy, depending upon your point of view.

> Woe betide the land when a slave has become its king, and its princes feast in the morning. Happy the land when its king is nobly born, and its princes feast at the right time of day, with self control, and not as drunkards (Eccles. 10.16–17).

Another Proverb contrasts the lack of vision which leads to an undisciplined people with the attitude of the person who keeps torah:

> . . . happy is he who keeps the law (Prov. 29.18b).[16]

The translation of Prov. 28.14 is a matter of dispute. The KJV renders:

> Happy is the man that feareth alway:
> but he that hardeneth his heart shall fall into
>   mischief.

The ending of the first line has been made more explicit in many modern translations – RSV and NIV 'fears the Lord'.[17] There is, however, little justification for this. The Hebrew word here translated 'fear' (*pahad*) comes close to the concept of 'dread' and is never found anywhere else in the wisdom literature linked to the name of God as a parallel to the normal expression 'the fear of the Lord'. The clue to the meaning here may be found in the use of the same verb in Jer. 36.24 where the absence of this 'fear' describes the callous insensitive attitude of Jehoiakim and his courtiers as they cut Jeremiah's scroll into pieces and drop the pieces into the fire. Unless the meaning of the verse is to be decided by the possible religious reference to confession in the previous verse there is a great deal to be said for the NEB rendering:

> Happy the man who is scrupulous in conduct,
> but he who hardens his heart falls into misfortune.

The one occurrence of an *'ashre'* saying in the book of Job is to be found on the lips of Eliphaz as he seeks to defend the traditional wisdom thesis that tragedy and disaster must be seen as a divine warning or part of God's discipline:

> Happy the man whom God rebukes!
> therefore do not reject the discipline of the Almighty (Job 5.17).

None of these passages does any more than underline the typical wisdom emphasis that there is a divinely given order built into life: to live in accordance with such order is the mark of wisdom and brings its own rewards, 'happy is the person who so lives . . .'

There is, however, one *'ashre'* saying in Proverbs which uses different language to strike a different note – Proverbs 16.20, well translated by McKane:

> He who is quick to take a point prospers,
> but happy is he who trusts in Yahweh.

'He who is quick to take a point' probably refers to the ability of the pupil to grasp what he is being taught by his wisdom teacher – this seems more likely than the NEB translation 'The shrewd man of business'. But what is the relationship of this intellectual quickness to 'trusting in the Lord'? Is this a plea for a fruitful partnership of intellectual acumen and religious piety; or is there an antithesis implied, namely that such 'trusting in the Lord' is a gift more to be desired than intellectual acumen?[18] Either way this is the only passage in the wisdom literature which links such happiness with 'trust in the Lord'. Indeed the expression 'trusting in the Lord' (Hebrew *batah* followed by the preposition 'b') occurs only once elsewhere in Proverbs, in 29.25 where it contrasts with the attitude of those who cringe before men.

When we turn, however, to the *'ashre'* sayings in the Psalms the picture is very different. For one thing such *'ashre'* sayings are much more numerous in the Psalms than in the wisdom literature, some twenty six occurrences as opposed to nine. They are not only more numerous, but significantly different and broader in scope. There are some *'ashre'* sayings in the Psalms which continue to move within the confines of the major interests of the wisdom teachers. Thus Psalm 1.1 declares: 'Happy is the man who does not walk in the counsel of the wicked.' It then proceeds to draw a sharp distinction between the wicked and the righteous, and their respective lot in life, a common theme in the wisdom literature (e.g. Prov. 4.18,19; 10.7). Psalm 127 regarding children, or at least sons, as a gift from the Lord, claims that 'Happy is the man who has his quiver full of them' (Ps. 127.5). Psalm 128 begins by picking up the wisdom theme of 'the fear of the Lord' and declares 'Happy are all who fear the Lord' (Ps. 128.1). It goes on to describe the prosperity which will ensue for such people:

> You shall eat the fruit of your own labours,
> you shall be happy and you shall prosper (verse 2).

The concluding section of Psalm 144 looks across a life crowned with numerous, attractive children, sons and daughters, well stocked granaries, healthy flocks of sheep and cattle, a life untroubled by distress of any kind, and ends:

> Happy are the people in such a case as ours;
> happy the people who have the Lord for their God (Ps. 144.15).

But it is here that we begin to sense that the *'ashre'* saying has been given a new context. We are no longer talking about the happiness which is the mark of a person who acts in a particular way; there is now a strongly corporate emphasis. We are talking about a community, a people to whom such happiness comes, a community whose identity is bound up with its relationship to God. Likewise Psalm 128, however strong its wisdom orientation, talks of the Lord's blessing coming from Zion, the centre of the nation's religious life and worship, and it ends with the words, 'Shalom (fullness of life) be upon Israel.' Psalm 89.15 declares:

> Happy are those who have learned to acclaim you (or who join in the joyful festival shouts, Hebrew *teru'a*)
> who walk, O Lord, in the light of your presence.

No longer are we in a wisdom school, listening to the verdict of a wisdom teacher and his characterization of the kind of life which is 'on the ball', we are with the community gathered for worship, joining in a great festival occasion, and in that context looking at what constitutes the good life. Into many of the *'ashre'* sayings in the Psalms there is gathered this joyful experience of worship in the temple. Psalm 65 begins with the people rendering due praise to the God who is in Zion, confessing their sins in his presence, and then declaring:

> Happy is the man of your choice,
> whom you bring to dwell in your courts;
> let us enjoy the blessings of your house,
> your holy temple (Ps. 65.4).

This note comes through very strongly in Psalm 84, that moving psalm in praise of God's house. After expressing the psalmist's heartfelt longing to be in the courts of the temple, it leaves us in no doubt as to where true happiness lies:

> Happy are those who dwell in your house;
> they never cease from praising you.
> Happy are the people whose refuge is in you – (Ps. 84.4,5a).

and it ends with the words:

> O Lord of Hosts,
> happy the man who trusts in you (Ps. 84.12).

Psalm 40.4 declares:

> Happy is the man who makes the Lord his trust,
> and does not look to brutal and treacherous men,

and then breaks into a joyful celebration of the great deeds that God has done for his people in the past, as the basis for an appeal for help in the present crisis.

It is as if the characteristic link between the *'ashre'* saying and wisdom has now been replaced by a link between the *'ashre'* saying and 'trusting in the Lord';[19] and not only a link with the Hebrew expression which lies behind 'trusting in the Lord', but also with other expressions which are moving within the same semantic field, notably with the expression 'finding refuge in the Lord' (Hebrew *hasah* followed by the preposition *'b'*). Thus Psalm 2 ends: 'Happy are all who find refuge in him.'

Psalm 34, a psalm with numerous wisdom motifs (see Chapter 3), nevertheless in typical cultic style asserts:

> Taste, then, and see that the Lord is good.
> Happy the man who finds refuge in him! (Ps. 34.8)

and this is echoed in its concluding words:

> . . . none who seek refuge in him are brought to ruin (verse 22).

Indeed it is this strong sense of a personal relationship with a living, ever present God which is the dominant context for the *'ashre'* sayings in the Psalms, and which differentiates them sharply from the *'ashre'* sayings in the wisdom literature:

> Happy is the man whom you instruct, O Lord,
> and teach out of your law . . . (Ps. 94.12)

and this because such a man belongs to a community which in worship confesses its faith that

> The Lord will not abandon his people
> nor forsake his chosen nation . . . (Ps. 94.14).

The same point can be made by looking at two passages in which the verb related to *'ashre'* is used, on each occasion in parallelism with the verb 'to praise'. In the poem 'The Golden ABC of the Efficient Housewife' which rounds off the book of Proverbs, it is said that because of her skill and competence

> Her sons with one accord call her happy;
> her husband too, and he sings her praises (Prov. 31.28).

Similarly in the Song of Songs 6.9 the bridegroom or lover, after waxing eloquent over the physical charms of his beloved, declares:

> Young girls see her and call her happy,
> princesses and concubines praise her.

There is however no parallelism in the Psalms between calling someone 'happy' and praising the positive qualities of that person – whether domestic efficiency, physical charm, moral attributes or the possession of wisdom. Instead Psalm 112 summons the people to worship with the words 'Praise the Lord' as the introit to the man who is described as *'ashre'*! The focus of interest has shifted from the horizontal analysis of human characteristics and conduct to the celebration of life centred upon God, to the vertical dimension of that confrontation with God which is the worshipper's experience. It remains to be seen what new dimensions, if any, this adds to the major issues with which the wise in Israel wrestled.

Chapter 3

Some Wisdom Psalms

We have looked at the way in which the *ashre* sayings in the Psalms take on a particular colouring, which differentiates them from similar types of sayings in the wisdom literature, a colouring which seems to be a reflection of their new context – the community of faith gathered for worship. Let us now try to broaden the scope of this approach by looking at a cluster of psalms, all of which at one time or another have been classified among the wisdom psalms, Psalms 32 and 34 regularly so, Psalm 33 more intermittently. Each of these psalms contains an *ashre* saying (32.1; 33.12; 34.9). On form-critical grounds, however, they represent a variety of types: Psalm 32 is usually treated as an individual thanksgiving psalm, Psalm 33 as a community hymn containing the same number of verses as there are letters in the Hebrew alphabet and Psalm 34 again as an individual thanksgiving psalm, but structured as an alphabetic acrostic, with one letter, the letter 'waw' omitted between verses 6 and 7 (English vv. 5 and 6). Although the superscription to Psalm 34 links it in a somewhat garbled way with an incident in the life of David – the king for whose benefit David feigned madness being Achish in I Sam. 21.10–15, not Abimelech – there is nothing in the psalm to suggest that it is a royal psalm and it is not usually classified as such. These three psalms are, therefore, very varied in type and in literary structure, but they all display clear links with the wisdom literature.

Psalm 32

At the heart of Psalm 32 there is the description in verses 3–5

(Eng.), of an experience of misfortune or suffering, whether physical or psychological we can hardly decide – it could indeed have been both – an experience which the psalmist regarded as divinely sent punishment upon his sins. Only through confession, and perhaps by undergoing some rite of absolution, did he find relief and new vitality. This link between suffering and sin, and the consequent need for confession, either corporate or personal, was widely held in the ancient world. To take but one example from the ancient Near East, there are the 'Plague Prayers of Mursilis' the Hittite Emperor in which, faced with his country ravaged by plague and threatened by external enemies, he pleads his own innocence but confesses to the Storm-god the sins of his father and asks that he and his people be made aware of any other offences which may have provoked the anger of the gods: 'O gods, whatever sin you behold, either let a prophet come and declare it, or let the sybils or the priests learn about it by incubation, or let man see it in a dream! . . . O gods, take pity again on the Hatti land'.[1] This is a recurring theme in the psalms (cf. 25; 38; 51), and it is equally there in the wisdom literature. It is this analysis of his tragedy and the necessary response to it which the friends repeatedly and increasingly urge upon Job. In his final speech Eliphaz, after cataloguing Job's offences (22.5–7), declares that this is the reason why:

> there are pitfalls all around you,
> and suddenly you are full of fear.
> It has grown so dark that you cannot see,
> and a flood overwhelms you (22.10–11).

He then makes his final appeal to Job:

Come to terms with God and you will prosper;
that is the way to mend your fortune . . .

If you come back to the Almighty in true
   sincerity. . .

Then, with sure trust in the Almighty,
you will raise your face to God;
you will pray to him, and he will hear you (22.21, 23, 26, 27a).

'Conceal your faults' says Proverbs 28.13, 'and you will not prosper; confess and give them up, and you will find mercy.' And the psalmist in Psalm 32 has put this to the test:

> I acknowledged my sin to thee,
> and I did not hide my iniquity;
> I said 'I will confess my transgressions to the Lord';
> then thou didst forgive the guilt of my sin (v.5).

Gripped by the reality and the wonder of this experience of confession and forgiveness he commends it to his fellow worshippers as something that they can and ought to share (vv.6–7).

Thus far we can see a common theme, part of a 'shared approach to reality', being handled by psalmist and wisdom teachers, and just as the wise sought to provide instruction on this theme to those who were prepared to listen to their teaching, so the psalmist seeks to share his experience as a way of instruction for his fellow worshippers. This experience of the psalmist, however, has in Psalm 32 been placed within an interesting framework.

(*a*) It is prefaced (verses 1–2) by two *ashre* sayings which seek to generalize the psalmist's experience. What is noteworthy about the first *ashre* saying is its form. It provides the only example in the Old Testament of *ashre* followed by a passive verb:

> Happy are those whose rebellion is forgiven,
> whose sin has been put away (v.1).

The people to be congratulated or considered 'happy' are no longer those who follow the right ways or who display a certain attitude to life – e.g. by fearing the Lord – as in Proverbs, but people to whom something has happened, people who have been on the receiving end of 'forgiveness' as that has come to them in worship. Equally the second *ashre* saying,

> Happy is a man when the Lord lays no guilt to his account,
> and in his spirit there is no deceit (v.2)

while not in the passive form, points to something which can only be received, the verdict of 'not guilty' that God passes on a human life. It is hardly surprising that Paul, with a faith firmly centred on God's grace and on what God has done for the human race in Christ, uses the opening of Psalm 32 to good effect in Romans 4.6ff. These introductory *ashre* sayings in Psalm 32, therefore, confirm and take a step further than our earlier analysis of the psalmists' linking of *ashre* with 'trusting in God' suggested, that the psalmists' use of *ashre* changes the essentially horizontal dimension of its wisdom use into a vertical dimension central to worship, in this case pointing strongly to an initiative which comes and can only come from God.

(*b*) The account of the Psalmist's experience and his call to others to share in it (vv. 3–7) lead into a piece of instruction (vv. 8–9) beginning with the words:

> I will instruct you and teach you the way you should go;
> I will counsel you with my eye upon you.

It has often been argued that this section of the Psalm is spoken in the name of God by a cultic prophet, the 'I' of verse 8 being God.[2] Thus the GNB inserts as an introduction to these words 'The Lord says'. There is, however, no hint in the text that the words should be taken as a divine oracle. What we are given is simply a piece of instruction, an invitation to learn, which in terms of imagery and vocabulary has close links with the wisdom literature.[3] If these verses had occurred in the book of Proverbs or in the book of Job no one would ever have dreamed of classifying them as anything other than typical wisdom teaching. Nor is there anything in the concluding two verses to contradict this strong impression of wisdom colouring. Verse 10 touches upon the long and deeply held view that the wicked (*resha*) experience trouble or torments, while a providential care or faithfulness (*hesed*) surrounds those who 'trust in the Lord', a characteristic psalmic experience (cf. Ps. 34). The wicked are then contrasted with the 'righteous' (*saddiqim*) and the 'upright in heart' (*yishre-leb*)[4] who are summoned to join in the joyful worship of God.

It would be hard to find a Psalm which more fully and effectively integrates wisdom and worship. Psalmist and wisdom teacher facing and responding to a common experience. The verdict of E. Gerstenberger is judicious: 'This Psalm comes very close to being a homily on penitence, a sermon preached from the life experience of the community, not so much from Scripture. Its theological reflection follows the lines of Job's friends and of much of the wisdom literature at that. The one who suffers should make an honest confession and then be redeemed.'[5] There is little reason, however, for accepting his view that the Psalm is based on synagogue preaching, finding its natural setting in the congregation of the faithful in early Judaism. It seems far more likely that the natural life-setting for Psalm 32 is the Jerusalem temple at an earlier, probably pre-exilic date. The fact that there is no mention of sacrifice in connection with the psalmist's confession and experience of forgiveness proves nothing. It is not the mechanism but the fact which is central to the psalmist's thinking. We might as well argue that the Psalm cannot be late since it does not contain any explicit reference to torah as scripture. There is nothing in the description of the worshippers as 'faithful', 'trusting in the Lord', 'righteous' and 'upright in heart' which necessitates a late date. It is important not to underestimate the *teaching* element in Israel's worship from an early period,[6] not simply teaching as in the recital of the past mighty acts of God in Israel's history or in creation (e.g. Psalm 136), but teaching on the fundamental questions of human life with which the wisdom teachers wrestled. Too little attention has been paid to this educative function of the cult, in a context where people are being reminded that they are not only searching but receiving, not only reaching out for God but being grasped by God.

Psalm 33

Psalm 33 may seem at first sight an unpromising field for investigation and it is only rarely treated as a wisdom psalm.[7] Apart, however, from Psalm 10, which, it is generally agreed, forms a literary unity with Psalm 9, it is the only psalm in the first collection (Pss. 1–41) which does not have a superscription of its own. This, plus certain strong linguistic similarities, suggests that it should be taken closely with Psalm 32 and that the compilers of the psalms probably saw it as fulfilling the same liturgical function as Psalm 32.

The Psalm begins (verses 1–4) with a typical call to worship (cf. Pss. 113; 135; 147; 150), such praise of Yahweh being the appropriate attitude of the 'righteous' and the 'upright', which is precisely the note on which Psalm 32 ends. The 'upright' (*yesharim*), as the description of a class of worshippers acceptable to God occurs frequently in the psalms, while the wisdom literature refers more than once to the liturgical acceptability of the 'upright'. Thus

The sacrifice of the wicked is an abomination to the Lord,
but the prayer of the upright is his delight (Prov. 15.8).

He who walks in uprightness fears the Lord,
but he who is devious in his ways despises him (Prov. 14.2).

The reiterated description of God-fearing Job as a man who is
'blameless and upright' (Job 1.1,8; 2.3), is matched by Bildad's
words to Job:

If you are pure and upright (*yashar*) surely then he (i.e. God)
will rouse himself for you and regard you with a rightful
habitation (Job 8.6).

In Psalm 33 the call to the upright to worship is rounded off by a
statement which provides the motivation for such worship:

For the word of the Lord is upright (*yashar*);
and all his work is done in faithfulness (v.4).

Descriptions of the Lord or the word of the Lord as upright
(*yashar*) are not common in the Old Testament and are virtually
confined to the psalms (cf. 25.8), to other liturgical passages (cf.
Deut. 32.4) and to the wisdom writings. The closest parallel to
this passage is to be found in Proverbs 8 where Wisdom in her
summons to men declares:

All the words of my mouth are righteous:
there is nothing crooked or twisted in them.
They are all straight to him who understands
and upright (*yashar*) to those who find knowledge (Prov. 8.8).

Psalm 33 then moves into a hymnic passage (vv. 5–7) which
celebrates Yahweh the God of Israel, with particular emphasis
upon his function as creator. This is the God who 'loves the
righteous' . . . by whose word 'the heavens were made' . . . who
'gathers the waters of the sea' . . . who 'puts the deeps in storehouses' (all hymnic participles). Now creation theology is by no
means confined to wisdom literature or to the Psalms in the Old
Testament (cf. Genesis 1, the Amos doxologies, Second Isaiah),
nevertheless it has a central place in wisdom thinking, witness in
particular the speeches of the Lord to Job in chapters 38–41, and it
reaches its climax in the great hymn of creation in Sirach 42.15–
43.33 which begins:

I will now call to mind the works of the Lord,
and will declare what I have seen.
By the words of the Lord his works are done (Sir. 42.15).

Within the Old Testament the closest parallels to the language of the psalm here are to be found in Job 38 where in verse 22 there are two references to God's 'storehouses' (*oseroth*), the storehouses of the snow and the storehouses of the hail,[8] and in verse 37 a reference to the 'waterskins' of heaven, which parallels in thought if not in language the 'bottle' or goatskin in which the sea is gathered in verse 7. Thus this hymnic section in Psalm 33, both in language and in theme, provides strong echoes of wisdom material.

The structure of the middle section of the psalm, verses 8–19, is not so easily analysed, and many different approaches to it have been suggested.[9] There is, however, much to be said for dividing it into three equal sections, each containing four lines of Hebrew poetry: (*a*) verses 8–11; (*b*) verses 12–15; and (*c*) verses 16–19. In each of these sections a clear didactic or instructional element appears.

(*a*) Verses 8–11: this section begins with an exhortation, a universal exhortation, to 'fear the Lord' and to 'stand in awe of him',[10] in the light of his effortless creative power; 'for he spoke and it came to be' (cf. Gen.1). It proceeds to contrast the 'counsel of the nations (*goim*)' and the 'thoughts (or plans) of the peoples (*amim*)' which the Lord frustrates, with the 'counsel of the Lord' and the 'thoughts (or plans) of his heart' which 'stand for ever'. A similar contrast is to be found in Prov. 19.21

Many are the thoughts (or plans) in the mind of man,
but it is the counsel of the Lord that shall be established
(cf. Job 12.13).

Wisdom concerns and phraseology are, therefore, well to the fore in this section.[11]

(*b*) Verses 12–15: this section opens with an *ashre* saying which like so many of the other *ashre* sayings in the psalms has been given a corporate reference: 'Happy is the nation whose God is the Lord, the people he has chosen for his possession'; happy in contrast to the nations and the peoples of the previous section

whose plans the Lord frustrates. The hymnic description of the
Lord who 'looks down from heaven. . . ' (vv.13–14), using
typical psalmic language, ends by portraying him as the one who
'fashions the hearts of them all, and discerns all their deeds' (v.
15). The only other passages in the Old Testament where this
verb 'discerns' (*bin*) is found with God as its subject are II Chron.
28.9 where Solomon is advised to seek the God of his father 'for
the Lord searches all hearts and discerns every plan and thought'
(and Solomon's connection with wisdom is central to Old
Testament traditions); Job 28.23 where God and God alone
discerns the way of wisdom; and Psalm 139.2 where the psalmist
confesses that God discerns his thoughts from afar. Such divine
discernment is, therefore, a characteristic of the wisdom and the
psalm traditions in the Old Testament.

(*c*) Verses 16–19: this section warns against false trust in human
power, very much in the vein of Isa. 30.15–16 and 31.1–2,
passages in which the prophet is probably attacking the pragmatic advice on current political issues being offered by some of
the 'wise' attached to court circles in Jerusalem namely, that
safety in face of the Assyrian threat was to be found in the
Egyptian military machine. The latter passage indeed asserts
that over against such advice it is the Lord who is 'wise' (*hakam*).
One of the implications of such divine wisdom is that the Lord is
in control of all that happens in human experience and history,
and his people should and can trust him (Isa. 31.4–9). The
psalmist's way of expressing this is to say:

> the eye (or eyes) of the Lord is on those who fear him
> (v.18),

a phrase which is very much at home in wisdom writings. So
Elihu claims:

> . . . his (i.e. God's) eyes are upon the ways of a man,
> and he sees all their steps (Job 34.21; cf. Prov. 22.12).

Outside the wisdom writings it is commonly found only in the
language of worship and prayer. In Psalm 66.7 God is described
as the God 'whose eyes keep watch on the nations', and Psalm
34.15 parallels the thought of Psalm 33 by claiming that 'The eyes
of the Lord are toward the righteous' (cf. Jer. 5.3).[12]

All of this, however, does not mean that this psalm simply falls into the category of wisdom instruction, at least not instruction as it is given in the context of a wisdom school. The Psalm ends where it began with the call to worship and the confession of faith by the worshipping community:

> We wait for the Lord;
> he is our help and shield.
> For in him our heart is glad,
> we trust in his holy name.
> Let your steadfast love, O Lord, be upon us,
> as we have put our hope in you (vv.20–22).

We note again, however, that wisdom teaching and instruction indissolubly blend with the call to worship and the confession of faith by the worshipping community. There is, moreover, nothing in my opinion to support the view that 'The apparent ecclesiastical organization is the diaspora community of the "right ones", the "upright" (v.11), the "elected" (v.12), the "God-fearing" and the "ones waiting for Yahweh's help (v.18), whom he saves from death and famine" (v.19), the ones "who long for and trust in the solidarity of Yahweh" (vv.20–22).'[13] None of these phrases is peculiar to the later diaspora communities: all of them can just as easily find a natural setting in the worship of the community attached to the Jerusalem temple prior to the exile.

Psalm 34

If Psalm 33 has very infrequently been offered membership of the Wisdom Psalm club, Psalm 34 may be described as part of the club's establishment, though it was not one of Gunkel's founder members. The reasons for its inclusion among the wisdom psalms are not hard to find. Formally it is an alphabet acrostic (omitting the letter *waw*; cf. Ps.25) and such acrostic poems are typical of liturgical material, laments, hymns and thanksgiving psalms, within the Psalter (e.g. Pss. 9/10; 25; 37; 111; 112; 119; 145) in the book of Lamentations and at home in the wisdom tradition (e.g. Prov. 31.10–31). Such acrostic poems are a recognized literary device elsewhere in the literature of the ancient Near East.[14] The overall structure of the psalm presents few, if any, major problems. After the superscription (see above) it opens (vv.1–3) with an invitation to join in the praise and adoration of God. Although there is no direct address to the Lord in the entire psalm (contrast Ps. 25.1; 30.1), the psalmist immediately invites his fellow worshippers to join with him in his praise of the Lord:

> O magnify the Lord with me,
> and let us exalt his name together! (v.3)

The language used here is very much psalm centred. 'Magnify' (piel of *gdl*) occurs only once elsewhere with God as the object and that is in Ps. 69.30:

> I will praise the name of God with a song,
> I will magnify him with thanksgiving

while 'exalt' (*rum*, polel) is commonly found in psalms in parallelism with words denoting thanksgiving (Ps. 118.28), worship (Ps. 99.5, 9), praise (Ps. 107.32) and blessing (Ps. 145.1). If, therefore, Psalm 34 is classified, as it sometimes is, as a Psalm of Thanksgiving of the Individual, it nevertheless from the outset has a strongly corporate and cultic orientation.

In verses 4–10 the psalmist describes the experience which prompted his thanksgiving, an experience of answered prayer, and of deliverance from 'all my fears' (the noun used here comes from the verbal root *grr* found in 33.8) and 'troubles'. What is noteworthy, however, about the way in which the psalmist tells his story is the switch he repeatedly and immediately makes from his own experience to calling upon others to share his experience and to prove for themselves that it is valid. Thus 'I sought the Lord and he answered me' in verse 4 leads into 'Look to him and be radiant' in verse 5[15] 'This poor man cried and the Lord heard him' in verse 6 leads into 'O taste and see that the Lord is good' in verse 8 and 'O fear the Lord, you his saints' in verse 9. This mixture of an appeal to experience followed by an admonition to the congregation is good liturgical practice, but it is also a familiar technique in the wisdom writings. It is part of the dialectic style which Job's friends repeatedly use in their attempt to bring him to his senses. This is how it is in our experience, they say, therefore, this is how you must react. Thus Eliphaz in his final speech in chapter 22 appeals to experience (vv.15–20) and this leads into a plea to Job:

Agree with God, and be at peace;
thereby good will come to you.
Receive instruction from his mouth,
and lay up his words in your heart (Job 22.21–22).

There are moreover two other features of this section with which a wisdom teacher would have felt very much at home: (*a*) the use of the *ashre* saying in verse 8b

Happy is the man who takes refuge in him (see ch.2).

(*b*) The threefold occurrence of the phrase 'the fear of the Lord' – 'The angel of the Lord encamps around those who fear him' (v.7), 'O fear the Lord, you his saints' (v.9), and 'those who fear him have no want' (v.9b).

All this may be no more than suggestive, but it is impossible to doubt the strongly didactic character and the wisdom flavour in the following instruction section which runs from verses 11–21.

1. The introductory words 'Come, O sons, listen to me' (verb '*shama*') are a customary wisdom form of address. It is a form which runs through Proverbs 1–9 with the address directed either to 'my son' (Prov. 1.8, 10; 2.1; 3.1, 11, 21; 4.10, 20; 5.1; 6.1, 20; 7.1) or to 'sons' (4.1; 5.7; 8.32 'my sons'), an address usually accompanied by the admonition to listen/hear (Heb. '*shama*'):

Hear, my son, your father's instruction,
and reject not your mother's teaching (1.8).

Hear, O sons, a father's instruction,
and be attentive, that you may gain insight (4.1).

And now, my sons, listen to me:
happy are those who keep my ways.
Hear instruction and be wise,
and do not neglect it (8.32–33).

This form of address is typical not simply of Israel's wisdom teachers, but also of wisdom teaching in the wider world of the ancient Near East, notably in Egyptian instruction where, as McKane says, 'What began as parental instruction based on the hereditary character of high political office was carried over into the schools where apprentice statesmen were trained, and the "my son" form of address was preserved in this scholastic setting.'[16] A similar shift from parental to non-parental wisdom instruction may well have taken place in Israel. This particular form of address is not found anywhere else in the Psalms, the nearest to it – and the only other occurrence in the Psalms where the call to listen is addressed to someone other than God – is in the opening words of Psalm 49:

> Hear this, all peoples!
> Give ear, all inhabitants of the world (Ps. 49.1).

a Psalm which has throughout a marked wisdom character and which we shall have occasion to discuss later.

2. The content of the instruction is summarized in the words:

> I will teach you the fear of the Lord (v.11b),

the umbrella under which much of the teaching in Proverbs shelters. Indeed the initial call in Prov. 1.8 for the son to listen to instruction is immediately preceded by the statement that:

> The fear of the Lord is the beginning of knowledge;
> fools despise wisdom and instruction (Prov. 1.7; cf. 9.10).

But it is not merely such a key motif which provides the thematic link between the instruction in Psalm 34 and the wisdom literature; every other element in the instruction points in the same direction. The rhetorical question in verse 12,

> What man is there who desires life,
> and covets many days, that he may enjoy good?

joins hands with the invitation of Wisdom in Proverbs 3.15–16:

> She is more precious than jewels,
> and nothing you desire can compare with her.
> Long life is in her right hand;
> in her left hand are riches and honour.

The particular aspects of wisdom which are uppermost in the mind of the teacher in this psalm are the moral aspects:

> Then keep your tongue from evil
> and your lips from uttering lies;
> turn from evil and do good,
> seek peace and pursue it (vv. 13–14).

These are issues which are of primary concern in the wisdom writings – a 'lying tongue' and a 'false witness' are two of seven things which the Lord hates and which are an abomination to him in Proverbs 6.16–19. Issues of life and death are in many wisdom passages linked to the tongue:

> Death and life are in the power of the tongue.
> and those who live it will eat its fruit (Prov. 18.21).

The person who is intent on evil:

> . . . listens to wicked lips;
> and a liar gives heed to the mischievous tongue (Prov. 17.4).

> A man of crooked mind does not prosper,
> and one with a perverse tongue falls into calamity (Prov. 17.20).

An antithetic proverb in 15.4 states:

> A gentle tongue is a tree of life,
> but perverseness in it breaks the spirit.

The closing section of the instruction (vv. 15–21) then develops at length the theme of the contrast between the 'righteous' (*saddi-qim*) and the 'wicked' (*resha'im*), and their respective fates, a theme which had been touched upon towards the end of Psalm 33 and which is a commonplace in the wisdom writings, e.g.

> The Lord is a stronghold to him whose way is upright,
> but destruction to evildoers.
> The righteous will never be removed,
> but the wicked will not dwell in the land (Prov. 10.29–30).

> The way of the wicked is an abomination to the Lord,
> but he loves him who pursues righteousness
> (Prov.15.9; cf.4.19; 11.30–31; 29.6).

It is the premise upon which the friends build their case against Job, and it receives classic expression in the words of Elihu in chapter 36. It is the mark of the justice of God and the right way in which he orders life that God

. . . repudiates the high and the mighty
and does not let the wicked prosper,
but allows the just claims of the poor and the suffering,
and does not withdraw his eyes from the righteous (Job 36.5–6).

Psalm 1, one of the latest wisdom psalms which now acts as an introduction to the psalter, develops the same picture. Here in Psalm 34 this theme is placed wholly in the context of that relationship with God which is central to the worshipper's experience:

> The eyes of the Lord are toward the righteous,
> and his ear toward their cry (v.15).

It was widely recognized of course that life did not always seem to follow this script. This forms part of the tension between the sufferer and his friend in what W. G. Lambert has called the Babylonian Theodicy.[17] When the friend insists that

> He who waits upon his god has a protecting angel,
> The humble man who fears the goddess accumulates great
>   wealth (11.21–22),

the sufferer can only complain that this has not been his experience of life:

> In my youth I sought the will of the god.
> With prostration and prayer I followed my goddess.
> But I was bearing a profitless corvee as my yoke.
> My god decreed instead of wealth destitution.
> A cripple is my superior, a lunatic outstrips me.
> The rogue has been promoted, but I have been brought low
> (11.72–77).

Wisdom thinkers were realists. They recognized that suffering and tragedy could come to the righteous, that they could be 'broken-hearted' and 'crushed in spirit' (Ps. 34.18). In such circumstances many of Israel's wisdom teachers, like some of their counterparts in the wider world of the ancient Near East, insisted that such afflictions of the righteous could only be a temporary deviation from the script. When caught in the cords of affliction the righteous could be sure of God's presence and of God's deliverance.

The Lord is far from the wicked,
but he hears the prayer of the righteous (Prov. 15.29).

When the wicked dies his hope perishes,
and the expectations of the godless come to naught.
The righteous is delivered from trouble,
and the wicked gets into it instead (Prov. 11.7–8).

Eliphaz and all Job's friends interpret Job's tragedy in this way. It is a divinely sent discipline, which a good man will accept as such in the certainty that there will come a happy ending:

Behold, happy is the man whom God reproves;
therefore despise not the chastening of the Almighty.
For he wounds, but he binds up;
he smites, but his hands heal.
He will deliver you from six troubles;
in seven there shall be no evil touch you (Job 5.17–19; cf. 8.5–7).

Zophar's words developing this theme in 11.13ff. provide an excellent parallel to Psalm 34.15–21. He begins with a conditional cry for help:

If you set your heart aright,
you will stretch out your hands towards him (i.e. God)
(v.13).

This leads into an assurance in verses 15–19 whose essence is to be found in the words:

You will have confidence, because there is hope;
you will be protected and take your rest in safety (v.18).

He ends with a warning:

But the eyes of the wicked will fail;
all the way of escape will be lost to them,
and their hope is to breathe their last (v.20).

Conditional cry for help . . . assurance . . . warning . . . So in Psalm 34 the conditional element having been sounded in verses 13–14, and being implicit in the contrast between the righteous and the wicked in verses 15–17, the righteous 'cry for help' comes in verse 17. This leads immediately into the confident assurance of deliverance and protection in verses 17b–20, and from there to the final warning:

> Evil shall slay the wicked;
> and those who hate the righteous will be condemned (v.21).

The major difference is in language, Psalm 34. 17–21 in particular using language which is more appropriate to the liturgical setting in which the psalm is at home. It is this liturgical setting which leads, as not infrequently in the psalms, into the final words which are best taken not as part of the instruction but as a climactic confession of faith by the congregation:[18]

The Lord redeems the life of his servants;
none of those who take refuge in him will be condemned (v.22).

The choice of Psalms 32–34 for analysis in terms of their wisdom content was not made simply, or solely, because they conveniently lie together as a block of material in the Psalter. These psalms have an interesting common feature when seen against a wisdom background. They represent the view of what we might term a self-confident strand within wisdom thinking, a strand which is still sure of the divine order built into life, and believes that anything that seems to run counter to such order (e.g. the suffering of the righteous) can be taken into account without seriously questioning that order or the character of the God who ordained and sustains it. They are closer in this respect to Job's friends than to Job. What such Psalms seem to do is to provide support for such a view by setting it within the context of worship and thus providing the comfort and the assurance which seem to verify it. That there were many within Israel who felt no need to probe further and found such an attitude in worship deeply satisfying we need not doubt. This is how worship functions – and positively – for many people today, reinforcing belief in the inherent goodness and order in life. But not all wisdom teachers were so optimistic. More radical voices of perplexity and protest were to be heard, and they too have left their mark on Israel's approach to worship.

Chapter 4

The Search for Meaning

There was screened recently on Sunday evenings in Scotland a twenty-four part TV religious series called 'The Quest'. It was an attempt to portray one man's spiritual Odyssey. Much of the programme was devoted each week to interviewing people, both from within and outwith the Christian church, who were presumed to have thought deeply about the questions that life today poses, against the background of the widely held conviction that the traditional Christian answers no longer make sense. Thus a Scottish philosopher–playwright described life as a mixture of 'farce and misery'; tragedy being no longer relevant as a description since tragedy presupposes the noble man who holds on to certain high beliefs in some kind of divine purpose suffusing life. There is little doubt that the search for meaning today takes new forms and faces new challenges in the light of the scientific, technological and intellectual revolution through which we are living. The more we become immersed in such questions today, however, the greater the temptation to assume that the search for meaning is something novel that has only arisen once commonly accepted certainties, enshrined in tradition, have been irrevocably shattered by modern knowledge. This is a quaintly 'unhistorical' attitude which ignores the extent to which there has always been a potential clash between belief and experience; a clash which some people have solved by asserting the priority of belief over experience, others by asserting the priority of experience over belief. Religion owes most to those who refuse to walk along either of these roads, who seek to reconcile belief and experience and in that context continue the search for meaning. It was Goethe who said: 'The deepest, the only theme of human history, compared to which all others are of subordinate importance, is the conflict of scepticism with faith.'[1] Let me modify that statement to suggest that the deepest, if not the only theme of religious history, compared to which all others are of subordinate importance, is the conflict which comes when faith realizes that it cannot live without scepticism, and scepticism acknowledges that it cannot live without faith.[2] To this ancient Israel bears eloquent witness both in its wisdom writings and in its approach to worship. Let us try to document the extent to which the search for meaning, as symbolized by questions such as 'why' and 'how long', is present in the thought of Israel and in the wider cultural environment of the ancient Near East.

We begin by looking briefly at the evidence for this in ancient Near Eastern documents other than the Old Testament, briefly because of the comparative paucity of the surviving material, but also briefly because this material moves within certain prescribed boundaries which the Old Testament was forced to call into question. From *Egypt* round about the end of the third millennium BCE comes a document usually referred to as 'A Dispute over Suicide', but perhaps more truly described as the 'Dialogue of a Man tired of Life with his "Ba"' (his 'alter ego' or his soul). Although the document is primarily concerned with death and life beyond death in the light of contemporary Egyptian mortuary cults, the issues are discussed against the background of a period of social upheaval when men were trying to come to terms with the breakdown of the established social order and were groping for new values in a world which seemed to be increasingly bereft of values. Thus the man voices his perplexity to his 'Ba' in the question 'To whom can I speak today?'

> To whom can I speak today?
> There are no righteous.
> The land is left to those who do wrong.
> To whom can I speak today?
> There is lack of a trusted friend;
> One has recourse to an unknown to complain to him.
> To whom can I speak today?
> There is no one contented of heart;
> The one with whom one went, he no longer exists.

To whom can I speak today?
I am laden with wretchedness,
For lack of a trusted friend.
To whom can I speak today?
The sin which treads the earth,
It has no end.[3]

The question 'To whom can I speak today?', with its implicit search for some kind of explanation of the problems that life is posing, is never answered. The man's 'Ba' merely points out that the mortuary cult is not particularly helpful in this respect and that he should 'pursue happiness and forget care . . . and set mourning aside'.[4] Similar advice is to be found in the 'Song of the Harper' against a background of similar perplexity:

Follow thy desire and thy good;
Fulfil thy needs upon earth, after the command of thy heart,
Until there comes for thee that day of mourning.[5]

The influence of the mortuary cult, which by way of acceptance or criticism seems to have dominated much discussion in Egyptian circles, effectively neutralizes issues which elsewhere were to become of pressing theological significance.

When we turn to *Mesopotamian* literature the situation is more fluid. In the text 'Man and his God', which has been described by S. N. Kramer as a Sumerian variation on the Job motif the thesis is propounded that 'in case of suffering and adversity, no matter how seemingly unjustified, the victim has but one valid and effective recourse, and that is to continually glorify his god and keep wailing and lamenting before him until he turns a favourable ear to his prayers. The god concerned is the sufferer's personal god, that is the deity who, in accordance with the accepted Sumerian credo, acted as a man's representative and intercessor in the assembly of the gods.'[6]

At two points in the text the man's complaints spill over into questioning. After protesting that his god has done nothing to thwart the conspiracy that unexpected enemies have mounted against him, he asks:

I the wise, why am I bound to the ignorant youths?
I the discerning, why am I counted among the ignorant?

Food is all about, (yet) my food is hunger.
On the day shares were allotted to all, my allotted
    share was suffering.[7]

Later in the text the man turns to make his plea to his god:

My god, you who are my father who begat me, (lift up) my
    face. . .
(How long) will you leave me unguided?[8]

The search for meaning is here; questions are asked: but it is a
search which operates within certain clearly defined limits,
which are almost inevitable given the polytheistic background to
the text. There cannot be any radical questioning of the structure
of existence; there can only be a plea to a personal god to use his
good offices on behalf of his client in the assembly of the gods
who ultimately decide the fate of men.

When we turn to Babylonian literature, to the text *Ludlul Bel
Nemeqi* 'I will Praise the Lord of Wisdom' I can do no better than
quote the words of W. G. Lambert: 'For a long time it had been
customary to refer to *Ludlul* as "The Babylonian Job", and so long
as knowledge was restricted to the second tablet such a description was justified. Seen now in a more complete form it will not
bear the title so readily. Quantitatively the greater part of the text
is taken up with showing how Marduk restores his ruined
servant, and only a small part with trying to probe the reason for
the suffering of the righteous. In places the writer deliberately
sheers away from plainly facing this problem because of its
blasphemous implications. Perhaps "The Babylonian *Pilgrim's
Progress*" would be a better title. Under the surface, however, the
writer is perplexed by the same problem as Job. The world is
ruled by the lord Marduk, from whom justice is expected by his
servants. Yet Marduk allows even the most devoted to suffer.
The author of *Ludlul* finds no answer adequate to solve this
mystery. All he can say is 'that though it be the lord who has
smitten, yet it is the lord who will heal'.[9] Indeed if this were
regarded as the Babylonian Job the remarkable thing about it
would be the lack of questioning. Complaint is clearly voiced.
Here is a man who is being treated as if he had neglected the
gods, whereas in fact he had been scrupulously religious.

To me prayer is discretion, sacrifice my rule.[10]

This being so he is confused and appalled. He can only conclude that the ways of the gods are inscrutable. After reviewing his own pious actions he comments:

> I wish I knew that these things were pleasing to one's god!
> What is proper to oneself is an offence to one's god,
> What in one's own heart seems despicable, is proper to
>   one's god.

Only in this context do we hear a series of puzzled and resigned questions:

> Who knows the will of the gods in heaven?
> Who understands the plans of the underworld gods?
> Where have mortals learnt the way of a god?[11]

But if the will of the gods is wholly inscrutable and the moral judgments that people make do not in any sense apply to the conduct of the gods, then no serious questioning is possible, and the search for meaning is meaningless.

Nor are we taken much further by the so-called *Babylonian Theodicy*, an acrostic poem of twenty-seven stanzas each containing eleven lines. It presents us with a very measured and polite dialogue between a sufferer and a friend – at least measured and polite when compared with the dialogue between Job and his friends – a dialogue which touches upon the apparent injustice in the world where the powerful oppress the weak and the gods do nothing to defend the powerless. In face of the sufferer's complaint the friend can only reiterate that what the gods decide is beyond human understanding '. . . the plan of the gods is remote'.[12] Nevertheless, men must live in the conviction that crime does not pay. When the sufferer pushes his argument that it is the strong, the unscrupulous and the wicked whose conduct is often approved by society, the friend can only agree and argue that this too is part of the will of the gods:

> Nurru, king of the gods, who created mankind,
> And majestic Zulummar, who dug out their clay,
> And mistress Mami, the queen who fashioned them,
> Gave perverse speech to the human race.
> With lies, and not truth, they endowed them for ever.[13]

The sufferer concludes by making a twofold appeal (*a*) to his friend: 'Help me, look at my distress: know it' and (*b*) to the heavenly powers that be:

> May the god who has thrown me off give help;
> May the goddess who has (abandoned me) show mercy,
> For the shepherd Samas guides the people like a god.[14]
>> (*Babylonian Theodicy*, 11.295–297)

There is in all of this a frank recognition that human expectations as to how things ought to be ordered within the divinely decreed structures of life have not been fulfilled. There is a search for meaning, but it takes mainly the form of complaint rather than the note of urgency and protest which was to become characteristic of such a search in Israel; and it admits of no serious questioning of the gods. Much of this indeed is close to the attitude outlined in the prologue to the book of Job, where, in response to having been bereft of livestock, herdsmen and family, Job says:

> Naked I came from the womb,
> naked I shall return whence I came.
> The Lord gives and the Lord takes away;
> blessed be the name of the Lord (1.21).

And when he himself is afflicted with running sores from head to foot, he responds to his wife's invitation to 'curse God and die' with the words:

> You talk as any wicked fool of a woman might talk.
> If we accept good from God, shall we not accept evil? (2.10)

When we turn, however, to the dialogue between Job and his friends we enter a very different world. Job begins by directing a series of challenging questions to his friends, questions which underline the sense of meaninglessness which grips him:

> Why was I not still-born,
> why did I not die when I came out of the womb? (3.11)

> Why was I ever laid on my mother's knees
> or put to suck at her breasts? (3.12)

> Why was I not hidden like an untimely birth,
> like an infant that has not lived to see the light? (3.16)

> Why should the sufferer be born to see the light?
> Why is life given to men who find it so bitter? (3.20)

> Why should a man be born to wander blindly,
> hedged in by God on every side? (3.23)

Throughout the dialogue questions to the friends never cease. In response to Eliphaz' plea in ch.5 that he should trust God and patiently wait for God to restore him, Job retorts:

> Have I the strength to wait?
> What end have I to expect, that I should be patient? (6.11)
> Oh, how shall I find help within myself? (6.13)

In chapter 13 he returns to the attack, questioning the credentials of the friends to speak on behalf of God:

> Is it on God's behalf that you speak so wickedly,
> or in his defence that you allege what is false? (13.7; cf.16.8–9)

The harshly unsympathetic attitude of the friends provokes him into asking:

> Why do you pursue me as God pursues me?
> Have you not had your teeth in me long enough? (19.22)

When Zophar seeks to press home the argument that human experience from beginning to end proves that:

> the triumph of the wicked is short-lived,
> the glee of the godless lasts but a moment (20.5),

Job counters with the question:

> Why do the wicked enjoy long life,
> hale in old age, and great and powerful?
> (21.7; cf.16.17)

a theme which he develops at length in ch.24 where he graphically describes the wicked prospering at the expense of the orphan, the widow and the poor to whose prayers God pays no attention. He caps his presentation of this theme with the question:

> If this is not so, who will prove me wrong
> and make nonsense of my argument? (24.25)

Questions in abundance to his friends, but equally questions,
sometimes the same questions directed at God. Thus the question to his friends in 3.11: 'Why did I not die when I came out of
the womb?' is reshaped as a question to God in 10.18, 'Why didst
thou bring me out of the womb?' This is only one of a series of
questions to God which echo across ch.10, questions aimed at
dissecting the character of God and casting doubt on the justice of
the ways in which he works in the world:

> Do you find any advantage in oppression,
> in spurning the fruit of all your labour
> and smiling on the policy of wicked men? (10.3)

> Are your days as those of a mortal
> or your years as the life of a man,
> that you look for guilt in me
> and seek in me for sin,
> though you know that I am guiltless
> and have none to save me from you? (10.5ff.; cf.4.9b, 10)

Later he faces God with the demand for answers to two crucial
questions:

> How many iniquities and sins are laid to my charge?
> let me know my offences and my sin (13.23)

and

> Why do you hide your face
> and treat me as an enemy? (13.24)

Stressing the brevity and frailty of human life, Job wonders why
God should display such a marked and hostile interest in him:

> Do you fix your eyes on such a creature,
> and will you bring him into court to confront you? (14.3)

He seeks to undermine what he can only regard as the specious
arguments of his friends by asking:

> Can any man teach God,
> God who judges even those in heaven above? (21.22)

It is as if he is saying to the friends, you have produced an interesting lesson on how God works or is supposed to work, it is a pity *he* is not prepared to learn the lesson! All the puzzled bewilderment, the desperate search for enlightenment by a man who believes that nothing that he has done can possibly justify the extent of his present suffering and his lapse into a life devoid of meaning, break forth in a series of combative questions in chapter 31:

> What is the lot prescribed by God above,
> the reward from the Almighty on high?
> Is not ruin prescribed for the miscreant
> and calamity for the wrongdoer?
> Yet does not God himself see my ways
> and count my every step? (31.2–4)

Job seems to be accusing God of a miscarriage of justice, based on ignorance.

Not that Job has a monopoly of questions. When Elihu enters the debate he throws a barrage of questions at Job, notably in 35.1–8 and in 37.15–20, questions which seek to hammer home to Job the limitations of his knowledge and power over-against a God before whom all men must show reverence and fear (cf.37.24). But even Elihu is in this respect but a pale precursor of the Grand Inquisitor, the Lord himself who, out of the whirlwind, beats Job into the ground with question upon ironic question, beginning with the challenge:

> Who is this whose ignorant words
> cloud my design in darkness?
> Brace yourself and stand up like a man;
> I will ask the questions, and you shall answer (38.2–3).

Relentlessly the questions pour forth:

> Where were you when I laid the foundations of the earth? (38.4)
>
> Who settled its dimensions? (38.5; cf. 6,8,25)
>
> Have you taught it (i.e. the sea) to grasp the fringes of the earth? (38.13; cf. 16, 17, 18)
>
> Can you bind the cluster of the Pleiades
> or loose Orion's belt? (38.31; cf. 32, 34)

> Do you know . . . ? (39.1)

> Does your skill teach the hawk to use its pinions?
>   (39.26; cf.27).

Throughout the book of Job question is answered by question, and at the heart of the questioning, both as its object and as its subject, stands God. The search for meaning focusses upon God, the one and only God for the book of Job, the God whom Job insists must at least be just, and it forces God, in terms of the imagery of the book, to break his silence. When God does break the silence he is no more kid-gloved in his approach to Job than Job has been in his approach to God. Lest there be any lingering doubt as to the validity of Job's questioning not only of the friends' traditional wisdom stance but also of God, the epilogue, with supreme irony, has the Lord say to Eliphaz: 'I am angry with you and your two friends, because you have not spoken as you ought about me, as my servant Job has done' (42.7) – a curious verdict on those who had been respectfully defending the ways of God in face of the hectoring attacks of a distraught mind. But the book of Job is pointing us unambiguously to the central place that questioning had in the search for meaning in certain wisdom circles in Israel.

But if this be true of certain wisdom thinkers and writers in Israel, it is also abundantly true of Israel's approach to worship as this is reflected in the Psalms. Indeed the voice of questioning is heard more frequently in the Psalms than in the book of Job, and in Psalms of very varied type.[15] This is one of the areas in which it makes sense to talk of 'a shared approach to reality' between the wisdom tradition and the Psalms, a shared approach which takes us far beyond the wisdom psalms as narrowly defined. To focus the discussion solely on questions directed to God, there is the echoing 'why?' (*lamah*) in the face of incomprehensible suffering or tragedy befalling either the community or the individual.

> Why dost thou stand afar off, O Lord?
> Why dost thou hide thyself in times of trouble?
>   (10.1; cf.88.14; Job 13.24)

> My God, my God, why has thou forsaken me?
> Why art thou so far from helping me, from the
>   words of my groaning? (Ps.22.1)

I say to God, my rock:
'Why has thou forgotten me?
Why go I in mourning because of the oppression of the enemy?'
(42.9; cf.43.2)

Rouse thyself! Why sleepest thou, O Lord?
Awake! Do not cast us off for ever!
Why dost thou hide thy face?
Why dost thou forget our affliction and oppression?
(44.23, 24)

O God, why dost thou cast us off for ever?
Why does thy anger smoke against the sheep of thy
pasture? (74.1; cf.v.11)

Why should the nations say 'Where is their God?'
(79.10; 115.2)

There is the urgent 'how long'? (*ad ma; ad mathi; ad ana*):

> My soul also is sorely troubled.
> But thou, O Lord – how long? (6.3)
>
> How long, O God, is the foe to scoff?
> Is the enemy to revile thy name for ever? (74.10)
>
> O Lord, God of hosts,
> how long wilt thou be angry with thy people's
> prayers? (80.4)
>
> How long, O Lord, wilt thou hide thyself for ever?
> How long will thy wrath burn like fire? (89.46)

There are the direct puzzled questions (*ha*):

> What profit is there in my death,
> if I go down to the Pit?
> Will the dust praise thee?
> Will it tell of thy faithfulness? (30.9)
>
> Will the Lord spurn for ever,
> and never again be favourable?
> Has his steadfast love for ever ceased?
> Are his promises at an end for all time?
> Has God forgotten to be gracious?
> Has he in anger shut up his compassion? (77.7, 8, 9)

Wilt thou be angry with us for ever?
Wilt thou prolong thy anger for all generations?
Wilt thou not revive us again,
that thy people may rejoice in thee? (85.5, 6)

Dost thou work wonders for the dead?
Do the shades rise up to praise thee?
Is thy steadfast love declared in the grave,
or thy faithfulness in Abaddon?
Are thy wonders known in the darkness,
or thy saving help in the land of forgetfulness?
                                      (88.10, 11, 12)

From this sampling of a much larger body of questions in the
Psalms it should be evident that for Israel worship provided the
context not merely for adoration, the praise of God and confession, but also for the search for meaning, for the wrestling with
questions which were also the legitimate concern of the wisdom
writers. To eliminate such questions is to distort the Psalms and
to cloak Israel's worship in a seamless garb of piety which it never
wore. Worship was not only for those who had found, but also
for those who were seeking; not only for those for whom faith
was easy and natural, but also for those for whom it was difficult
and strange in the light of the unavoidable questions which
experience forced them to ask; not only for those who gathered
joyfully to sing 'Hallelujah', but for those who felt the need over
and over again to ask 'Why?'. But to bring such questions to
worship was to put them in a different context from that of the
discussions and the debates in wisdom circles; and it is important
to ask what difference, if any, this makes to the questions. Part of
the answer to this will only become clear – or clearer – when we
turn to consider more specifically in the next chapter the problem
of theodicy, but a few general comments may be in place here.

1. In worship the search for meaning is essentially a shared
experience, not merely shared in the sense of worrying at or
teasing out issues or tossing an argument to and fro, as in Job, but
shared with fellow worshippers who to a greater or lesser extent
are committed to the same search *in the presence of God*. Let me try
to illustrate this by two examples.

(*a*) Three times in the Old Testament the question is addressed
to God, 'What is man?' – once in Job 7.17 and twice in the Psalms,

Psalm 8.4 and 144.3. It is usually argued that Job 7.17 is a bitter parody of Psalm 8, 'a classic of irony in biblical literature'.[16] This may well be true, though it does depend upon certain assumptions being made about the comparative dating of Psalm 8 and the book of Job. Certainly Job's words: 'What is man, that thou makest much of him' (or 'exalt him', Heb. *gdl*) seem to echo the high place given to man in Psalm 8.5 where man has been made 'a little less than God' and crowned with glory and honour; while the phrase 'dost visit him every morning' (Job 7.18) contains a play on the ambiguity of the Hebrew word *pqd* which can mean 'visit with gracious intention' as in Psalm 8.5 where the RSV translates 'care for him', or as in this passage in Job 'visit' in the sense of harassing or punishing, a meaning underlined in verse 20 where 'That terrible phrase . . . "man watcher" spat out in fury completes the reversal of the Psalmist's view'.[17] Even if Job 7.17 is a bitter parody of Psalm 8, it should be remembered that from the time Job was written the two passages stood together in Israel's literature, the one in a wisdom book, the other in the Psalms, and the parody loses its point unless both passages were known. As such the two passages represent a very different approach not simply because the one speaks of a gracious God and the other of a hostile God, hounding man, but because of the context in which they occur. In Job 7 the wisdom context is not merely that of a man who is experiencing God's harassment and testing, but that of a man who wishes to be left alone to endure the brief tormented days which remain of his life, a man who looks forward to death as the doorway into a freedom where he will finally be rid of the God who hounds him:

> For soon I will lie in the dust;
> And you will seek me – but I will not be (Job 7.21).

When Psalm 144.3, echoing the thought if not the precise language of Psalm 8 asks:

> O Lord, what is man that thou dost regard him.
> or the son of man that thou dost think of him?

it is equally conscious of the frailty and the brevity of human life:

> Man is like a breath (Heb. *hebel*),
> his days are like a passing shadow (Ps. 144.4).

But this thought is placed in the context of a God who is described as:

> My rock and my fortress,
> my stronghold and my deliverer,
> my shield and he in whom I take refuge . . . (Ps. 144.2),

and it becomes the basis of an appeal to God to come, to act, to rescue and deliver (cf. vv.5–7). The question 'What is man?' in Psalm 8 evokes a sense of wonder; in Psalm 144 it evokes a sense of total dependence upon God, in Job 7 it is the cry of a man who wishes to eliminate God from his tortured life. The Psalms indicate responses appropriate to worship, since they set the question in the context of belief in a living God who comes to his people to give meaning to their existence and to answer human need: Job indicates a response which can ultimately only lead to the death of worship, since it is the cry of someone obsessed, understandably, with himself and his own problems, who wishes to be rid of God.

(*b*) Let us now look briefly at Psalms 42 and 43 which in fact form one psalm. The identity of the psalmist is uncertain. He may be a king, he may be an otherwise unidentified individual. At the centre of the Psalm stands a crisis situation in the psalmist's life which has been interpreted as defeat and banishment from Jerusalem or nearness to death or both.[18] Surrounded by people who pour scorn on his faith by asking mockingly 'Where is your God?' (42.3, 10), the psalmist turns questioningly to God:

> Why hast thou forsaken me?
> Why go I mourning because of the oppression of the enemy?
> (42.9 and with slight variation 43.2)

But his problem is not merely intellectual; it is highly personal and emotional. He recalls how once he had joined those who thronged to the temple, joyfully to worship and to praise God. Now he plumbs the depths of despair:

> Why art thou cast down, O my soul,
> and why art thou disquieted within me?

a cry which is heard three times in the Psalm – 42.5, 11; 43.5. On each occasion the cry is immediately countered by a statement pointing to a faith which is still reaching out to God:

. . . yet I will wait for God;
I will praise him continually, my deliverer, my God
(42.5, 11; 43.5).[19]

Thus puzzled questioning, despair and hope, the despondent seeker and the joyful worshipping community stand side by side within the Psalm, interacting upon one another. The questions are real and urgent; but so is the memory of the joyful worshipping community. The despair is almost overwhelming, but there still remains a hope which reaches out to God. For the psalmist God can never be merely the object of his questioning, since he is the living God who takes the initiative in response to his people's need. The search for meaning is here incorporated into the experience of worship. But may not this also become a two-way traffic – the experience of worship spilling over into the wise men's discussions and problems? Let me tentatively suggest that the God of the book of Job who is on the receiving end of Job's questions becomes the God who asks the questions in chapters 38–41, because the man who wrote these chapters believed in the reality of God's initiative, a reality communicated to him through worship. The language of these chapters indeed has close links with some of the great hymns of creation within the psalter. If Job 7.17 is a bitter parody of Ps. 8, Job 38–41 consciously draws upon Israel's hymns which celebrate God as creator.

2. We have been discussing and trying to illustrate the form which the search for meaning takes in the context of worship and belief in the God who comes to his people in worship, but suppose there is no such experience? Here it is worth pondering certain aspects of that most tantalizing of Old Testament books, the book of Ecclesiastes or Koheleth, to stick to his Hebrew name. It too is a wisdom book, the fruit of a man's frustrating search for meaning. The questions we hear in this book, however, are somewhat colder, more objective than the hurt cries which we hear in Job and in the Psalms. They fall into two main categories. There are first, the 'who knows?' or 'who can do X?' types of questions. In face of the common fact of death which comes to man and beast alike, Koheleth says 'Who knows whether the spirit (or breath) of man goes upwards or whether the spirit (or breath) of the beast goes down to the earth?' (3.21). Better make the most of the present, says Koheleth, 'For who can bring him

(i.e. anyone) through to see what will happen next?' (3.22). 'Who knows what is good for man in this life. . . ? Who can tell a man what is to happen next under the sun?' (6.11, 12). As for wisdom it is remote, beyond our grasp, deep, 'Who can discover it?' (7.24). 'Who is like a wise man? and who knows the meaning of anything?' (8.1). In all such questions Koheleth is stressing that the search for meaning takes you to certain frontiers beyond which it is impossible to go with any certainty, and he is highly sceptical of any claims to have cracked the code of the way in which God has ordered life: 'However much a man may try, he will not find out: the wise man may think that he knows, but he will be unable to find the truth of it' (8.17).

There is secondly a series of questions which centre upon the pointlessness of human life or of certain human activities, questions introduced by the phrase 'what profit is there?' or 'what does a man gain by. . .?' (Heb. *ma yithron*). Thus – 'What does a man gain from all his labours and all his toil here under the sun?' (1.3; cf.2.22), or 'What advantage . . . in facing life has the wise man over the fool?' (6.8). 'The more words one uses, the greater is the emptiness of it all: and where is the advantage to a man?' (6.11). The 'whys?' are also heard, but they are 'whys?' moving within a restricted field, calling into question the validity of certain courses of action. If, for example, one fate, i.e. death, befalls the wise and the fool alike 'Why should I be wise?' (2.15). If excessive conduct of any kind leads to ruin 'Why destroy yourself?' (7.16) by being self-righteous or over-wise, and 'Why die before your time?' by being excessively wicked.

While much of this seems to be the product of a shrewd, coolly analytic mind, it is not, I think, unrelated to the place of worship in this man's life. Koheleth's attitude to worship is contained in one key passage, 5.1 (Heb. 4.17) –7. Koheleth has in many respects a typically conservative mind and here as elsewhere he draws upon traditional teaching. His words about the priority of obedience over sacrifice echo prophetic teaching, I Sam. 15.22, and wisdom teaching, e.g. Prov. 21.3 'To do righteousness and justice is more acceptable to the Lord than sacrifice.' Never forget that, when you go to worship, says Koheleth. Likewise his remarks on making vows to God and meaning what you say when you make them, echo almost verbatim the teaching of torah in Deut. 23.21a 'When you make a vow to the Lord your God do

not delay to fulfil it . . .' And if in 5.2, in the words 'Do not rush
into speech . . .' he is merely advocating a sensible verbal
economy in worship, then all who have had bitter experience of
its opposite can only applaud his sentiments. But there is more to
it than this. Why should your words be few when you worship?
Because 'God is in heaven and you are on earth' (5.2). If this is
merely an attempt to stress the transcendence, the sovereignty
and freedom of God over against man, than it is unexceptional
theology and finds its counterpart in Psalm 115 where in
response to the mocking cry of the nations 'Where is their God?'
the answer comes:

Our God is in heaven; he does whatever he pleases (Ps. 115.3).

There is so much else, however, in Koheleth which points us in
a different direction. The God in whom he believes is a God
whose purposes are not only unchangeable but also unknowable (3.14). The words 'God is in heaven and you are on earth'
point to an unbridgeable gulf which separates Koheleth from
God. He advocates a wise caution so as not to give offence in
worship, but he shows no enthusiasm for worship. We can
hardly imagine him joining the joyful throng flocking to the
temple to shout 'Hallelujah'. He would probably have died with
embarrassment. For Koheleth the experimental side of religion
as mediated in worship seems to have died. He is left with a
God in whom he believes, a God whom he must respect ('fear
the Lord'), but a God who evokes neither devotion nor enthusiasm, and who is no longer impinging in any direct sense
upon Koheleth's life. Religion as exemplified in the Psalms has
been replaced by religious etiquette. God has been banished to
heaven, and this God gives Koheleth neither harassment nor
refuge. He is no longer a God who is in any danger of interfer-
ing. Koheleth's search for meaning leads him to that emptiness
(NEB), that meaninglessness (NIV), to that unanswerable
question mark which hangs over the whole of life which is
enshrined in his favourite phrase *'hebel habalim'*, 'vanity of
vanities'.

Worship untouched by the harsh questions that experience
brings would, in the light of the psalms, hardly be true worship,
but merely a form of escapism. But equally the harsh questions of

life, untouched by the rich vitality of worship, lead Koheleth to the abandoning of the search for meaning. It is when the concerns of the wise and the psalmists join hands that the search for meaning becomes and remains fruitful.

Chapter 5

The Problem of Theodicy

The word 'theodicy' as commonly used in philosophical and theological discussion was coined around 1700 CE by Gottfried Wilhelm von Leibnitz in his defence of the goodness and omnipotence of God in face of the existence of evil, whether metaphysical, physical or moral.[1] The term has been defined[2] as (a) vindication of the divine attributes, especially justice and holiness, in respect to the existence of evil, and (b), a writing, doctrine or theory intended to justify the ways of God to man; or, more loosely, as 'the attempt to pronounce a verdict of "Not Guilty" over God for whatsoever seems to destroy the order of society and the universe.'[3] But does such an undertaking 'the attempt to pronounce a verdict of "Not Guilty" over God' have any place at all in the faith of the Old Testament, or is it, as some have argued, the very antithesis of what faith, in the biblical sense, means? W. Eichrodt argued that '. . . theodicy was not fruit which had grown upon the tree of biblical faith in God, but was largely derived from the Stoic-Neoplatonic world view . . . Thus the question suggests itself: whether the distinctive character of Old Testament faith in God necessarily leads to a concern with theodicy, or whether such a notion proves to be a foreign element which cannot be assimilated by the forces which gave rise to Old Testament faith.'[4] It was as such a foreign element, inherently impossible within a faith based on revelation, that Eichrodt sought to handle the problem of theodicy. Thus while a recent series of Gifford lectures claims that the author of Job was 'the greatest of all the poets of theodicy',[5] and that in terms of the book 'the real theodicy is in the words of the divine voice',[6]

Eichrodt claims that the divine speeches in Job along with the hymn of creation in Genesis 1 'are a decisive protest against a theodicy which, by ostensibly seeking to justify the Lord of the world, placed him on the same level as the world and made him into an object of knowledge.'[7] Behind Eichrodt's verdict there seems to be the view that theodicy is a purely intellectual game, and that, as such, it is incapable of exploring the depths of the meaning of faith or revelation. But this is to box theodicy into too narrow a space, perhaps a comfortingly narrow space, since it leaves ample room for faith to flourish outside and to look with pity upon those trapped within questions and difficulties which would not exist for them if only they truly believed in the God of Israel. On this thesis it is hard to see why there should be so much in the Old Testament reflecting the views of those who *from within the context of Israel's religious traditions* found it hard to understand or to justify the ways of Israel's God.[8]

For the problem of theodicy to arise with any seriousness there are three essential preconditions: (1) there must be a firmly held belief in a coherent divinely-given order or structure of existence, an order or structure which makes sense in terms of human criteria of justice or rightness, (2) certain situations or experiences in life arise which call this belief seriously into question, and (3) current explanations of the tension, thus created, are deemed to be not only inadequate but misleading, whether such explanations speak in terms of divine retribution or of human sinfulness, be it deliberate or unwitting. Given these preconditions the problem of theodicy becomes acute to the extent to which people are prepared to push the question 'why?' to the limits of human understanding – an issue which we touched upon in the previous chapter. When we turn to the world of the ancient Near East outside Israel it is precisely because these three interlocking conditions do not give definitive shape to religious thinking that the problem of theodicy does not become acute.

In ancient Egypt, as we have seen, we have ample evidence for voices of complaint, deploring the injustice of a social order which does not protect or reward the upright and the pious, but allows the wicked to prosper.[9] There is, however, little real shaping of such complaints into 'whys?' which seriously question the whole concept of a divinely-given order. There seem to have been two reasons for this. In the first place the concept of law and order was too closely identified with the ruling Pharaoh, the god-king. His will was paramount and not subject to the scrutiny of his people. We can hardly envisage in ancient Egypt anything corresponding to the clash between Nathan and David (II Sam. 12) or Elijah and Ahab (I Kings 21), with the prophet insisting that there are certain absolutes in terms of justice which not even the king may dare to violate. If, in ancient Egypt, there is injustice, if the righteous experience suffering, then the fault cannot lie with Pharaoh or with the gods, but with the perversity of human nature.

The Instruction of King Amen-em-het to his son (circa 1900 BCE) has a lot to say about the disturbed times in which he lives, and about an attempted coup d'etat. He warns his son and successor against trusting even his own servants:

> It was he who ate my food who raised troops against me and he to whom I had given my hands that created terror thereby.[10]

But like similar Egyptian documents, this raises no questions as to why this should happen, or why the gods allow it to happen. As the much later Instruction of Ani says:

> Make offerings to thy god and beware of sins against him . . .
> Let thy eye have regard to the nature of his anger and prostrate thyself in his name. He shows his power in a million forms. (Only) they are magnified whom he magnifies. The god of the land is the sun which is on the horizon, and (only) his images are upon this earth.[11]

But doubts about the power or character of this sun-god are hardly in place and he is not subject to human questioning. This impression is supported by the mood of the great hymns to Amon, hymns which celebrate not only the creative and sustaining power of Amon Re, but also his function as the divine healer:

> He who dissolves evils and dispels ailments . . . Amon. Rescuing whom he desires, even though he be in the Underworld; who saves (a man) from Fate as his heart directs. To him belong eyes as well as ears wherever he goes, for the benefit of him whom he loves. Hearing the prayers of him who summons him, coming from afar in the completion of a moment for him

who calls him. He makes a lifetime long or he shortens it. He gives more than that which is fated to him whom he loves.[12]

What we do not hear are the cries of those whose prayers the god did not answer, or the complaint of those to whom he did not come when called. So long as men can be blamed for all that goes wrong, the gods remain serenely aloof and need not be too closely scrutinized. One suspects that Egyptian thought, allowing for the totally different cultural context and theological tradition, would not have been too unhappy with Milton's approach in Paradise Lost, written specifically to justify the ways of God to man, an approach in which a major part of his argument is that God created man with free will, and that it is the abuse of that free will which leads to suffering and tragedy. Into the mouth of God in Book III he puts the following words:

> They therefore as to right belong'd,
> So were created, nor can justly accuse
> Ther maker or ther making or ther Fate;
> As if Pre-destination over-ruled
> Ther will, disposed by absolute Decree
> Or high foreknowledge; they themselves decreed
> Ther own will, not I.[13]

But if neither 'Ther maker' nor 'ther making' nor 'ther Fate' can be accused then the problem of theodicy has been solved or side-stepped.

The second reason for the lack of any serious wrestling with the problem of theodicy in Ancient Egypt lies in the dominance of the mortuary cults. If there is any significant belief in life hereafter and the possibility that, for some at least, the seeming injustices of this world will be rectified in the next, then the sting is drawn from certain questions. Even when certain aspects of the mortuary cults are under attack, the influence of this way of thinking lives on.[14] Mainstream Old Testament wisdom tradition has no such escape route. We shall explore this issue more fully in the next chapter; let me simply draw attention at this point to the fact that as late as the second century BCE Jesus ben Sirach reflects the view that death is simply a step into that negation of all that makes life meaningful, the gloom and oblivion of Sheol:

Man's body wears out like a garment;
for the ancient sentence stands: You shall die.
In the thick foliage of a growing tree
one crop of leaves falls and another grows instead;
so the generations of flesh and blood pass
with the death of one and the birth of another.
All man's works decay and vanish,
and the workman follows them into oblivion (Sir. 14.17–19).

Proper burial and respect for the dead is in place, says Sirach, but not prolonged or excessive grief:

Never forget! there is no return;
you cannot help him and you can only injure yourself.
Remember that his fate will also be yours:
'Mine today and yours tomorrow'.
When the dead is at rest, let his memory rest too;
take comfort as soon as he has breathed his last (Sir. 38.21–23).

When we turn to Mesopotamian literature, the problem, as we saw in the last chapter, hinges upon the highly polytheistic colouring of the documents and the belief that ultimately the plans and thoughts of the gods are inscrutable, and therefore not subject to any evaluation in terms of what is considered to be just or good by men.[15] In the *Sumerian Lament over the Destruction of Ur*, we find Ningal, goddess of Ur, wife of the moon god Nanna, twice taking her tears and her complaints to the great council of the gods who had decided upon the fate of Ur:

To Anu the water of my eye verily I poured;
To Enlil I in person verily made supplication.
'Let not my city be destroyed' verily I said unto them;
'Let not its people perish' verily I said unto them.
Verily Anu changed not this word;
Verily Enlil with his 'It is good; so be it' soothed
                                        not my heart.[16]

The poem ends with a prayer addressed to Nanna that he may look favourably upon his people, accept their offerings and prayers and restore Ur to its former glory. In such a context gods may be asked to justify their decisions to other gods – though the most powerful gods are under no constraint to do so – but they do not need to justify their ways to man. Although later Babylonian literature e.g. *ludlul Bel Nemeqi*, is more reflective than the earlier Sumerian material, and gives voice to human complaint and protest[17] nevertheless the same dilemma remains. Man can only make his plea to his patron god or goddess in the hope that, in the face of personal or communal tragedy, the pleas of his god or goddess may prevail in the inscrutable council of the gods. Where there can be such divine 'passing of the buck' there is little likelihood of scope for radical human questioning of the divinely given structures of life, and no danger in the light of some of the patent anomalies of life, that you will be left asking with Abraham 'Shall not the judge of all the earth do what is just?' (Gen. 18.25).

Within the wisdom literature of the Old Testament and in the Psalms there is evidence for at least three ways in which attempts were made to side-step the problem of theodicy:

1. The legacy of the polytheistic background to Israel's thinking – and its continuing popular appeal – suggested a way through the problem by using the picture of the divine assembly, presided over by the one true God, the God of Israel, an assembly whose membership is now made up of lesser divine beings 'the sons of God' (Job 1.6) or 'the host of heaven' (I Kings 22.19) or 'the gods' (Ps. 82.1). Thus, however vehemently Job may insist in the dialogue with his friends that God is directly responsible for the tragedies which have befallen him – a God once a divine friend but now a cruel and capricious enemy – the Prologue takes a different line by asserting that the initiative came not from God, but from one of the 'sons of God' who, acting as counsel for the prosecution (the *Satan*), argues that Job's much vaunted piety can hardly claim to be disinterested. The prosecutor is given permission by God to turn the screws on Job. Although Job himself is blissfully unaware of this scenario the Prologue ends by affirming that the tighter the screws are turned, the more it becomes clear that God's confidence in Job is not misplaced. In face of affliction Job's response is one of unquestioning acceptance: 'Throughout all this, Job did not utter one sinful word' (Job 2.10). But if that is all then there is no problem of theodicy; God is in the clear. He has trusted Job and his trust is not misplaced.

Psalm 82 is even more daring, or naive, in its use of polytheistic concepts. There is no reason to doubt that the author of Psalm 82 believed in the God of Israel and the God of Israel alone, yet he depicts him as:

> Taking his stand in the council of the gods,
> to deliver judgment among the gods themselves (v.1).

This supreme judge then condemns these other gods to a most ungodlike fate:

> Gods you may be,
> sons all of you of a most high god,
> yet you shall die as men die;
> princes fall, every one of them, and so shall you (vv.6–7).

The reason for this fall from divine status and grace? These 'gods' are held to be responsible for the evil in the world, in particular for the injustice meted out to those at risk in society at the hands of the wicked. They are accused of being clueless as to the true moral basis on which the world ought to operate. Now this is theologically ingenious. It serves to stress the supreme power and the unique nature of Israel's God, while absolving him from any responsibility for the evil in the world – ingenious but hardly convincing. A theological magician is using sleight of hand to make the problem disappear, but while the audience may be temporarily baffled, or even convinced, the problem is still there unresolved.[18]

2. There is the attitude of those who deny that there is any problem, by insisting that life's experiences do not question the goodness or the power of God. In this, God's world, the righteous flourish, the wicked perish. When this does not seem to be the case, when in particular the righteous fall upon evil times, this must be accepted as a temporary discipline sent by a God who can be depended upon to restore the righteous to his favour. This attitude is found widely in Proverbs and in the Psalms (see chapter 3 and the discussion on Ps. 34); it is the stance of Job's friends. This is not merely theological blindness. It had such wide credence because it did correspond to many people's experience – and still does. At its most uncompromising this attitude is to be found in Psalm 37.25 where the psalmist declares:

I have been young and now I am old;
yet I have not seen the righteous forsaken
or his children begging for bread.

Put thus it invites contradiction. The New English Bible translators obviously found this too much to swallow. While they were prepared to leave the words, 'I have not seen the righteous forsaken', which could presumably be given a spiritual interpretation, they gave a free transfer to 'the children begging for bread' from verse 25, and the righteous, to verse 20 where they join the wicked:

But the wicked shall perish,
and their children shall beg for their bread.

This is by no means the only place where the NEB finds the Hebrew text theologically unacceptable and rewrites or reorders accordingly.[19] But we must allow Psalm 37 to say what it says, not what we might want it to say. Even in its revised NEB form the problem remains since the Psalm throughout insists that the wicked and their children perish, while the good and their children flourish (cf. vv.37–8). If this be so there need be no wrestling with the theodicy. As David Daiches puts it: 'If Milton could have accepted this, he would not have felt the need to write *Paradise Lost.*'[20]

3. There is no way of escape offered by Koheleth. Not for him belief in a sunny providence. His sky is often dark and clouded. He is well aware that in this world it is often the case that 'where justice ought to be, there was wickedness, and where righteousness ought to be, there was wickedness' (3.16). I saw, he says 'the tears of the oppressed, and I saw that there was no one to comfort them. Strength was on the side of their oppressors, and there was no one to avenge them' (4.1). Corruption he knows to be widespread. It is built into the bureaucratic system, and you can't beat the system (5.8). Wealth and prosperity simply bring their own problems – hangers-on, sleepless nights, a possible stock market crash, and the fact that not only can you not take it with you, but that you may have to leave it to an incompetent and idle fool (5.10ff.). Life is full of anomalies:

One more thing I have observed here under the sun: speed

does not win the race nor strength the battle. Bread does not belong to the wise, nor wealth to the intelligent, nor success to the skilful; time and chance govern all. Moreover no man knows when his time will come; like fish caught in a net, like a bird taken in a snare, so men are trapped when bad times come suddenly (9.11–12).

And at the end the inescapable fact of death: beyond it a great unknown (3.19–22). All of this, however, does not constitute for Koheleth a theological problem; it is simply fact. It does not raise serious questions about the character or purposes of God, because God is not only remote[21] but his purposes are unknowable. After the magnificent poem on the richly contrasting experiences of life, each with its appropriate time (3.1–8), he adds 'He (i.e. God) has made everything to suit its time; moreover he has given man a sense of time past and future, but no comprehension of God's work from beginning to end' (3.11). Providence there may be, 'but is it love or hatred? No man knows' (9.1). Instead of hammering uselessly on this closed door, says Koheleth, we are meant to get on with the business of daily living, and get as much out of it as we can. If Psalm 37 seeks to deny that there is a problem of theodicy by refusing to face realistically the existence of evil, Koheleth sidesteps it by refusing to allow God to be actively involved in the whole messy business. Koheleth's God is the Creator who has given us life to be enjoyed, even as we remember its frailty; he is a God to be feared and obeyed (5.7 and possibly 12.13), but he is not a God to whom ultimate questions can or ought to be directed, since we must accept that there are no answers.

There are, however, other voices in the Old Testament who refuse to accept that any of these approaches are adequate, and are thus forced to wrestle with the problems of theodicy at a deeper level.

It is because the author of the book of Job believes that the purposes and character of God can and must be put under human scrutiny that he becomes 'the greatest of all the poets of theodicy'. We have already noted (see chapter 4) how this leads Job to direct his urgent questions not simply to his friends but directly to God, angry agonizing questions to one who seems to be a sadistic torturer. He virtually accuses God of murdering an innocent victim. This is a God who not only condones evil, but who actively practises it:

> My enemies look daggers at me,
> they bare their teeth to rend me,
> they slash my cheeks with knives;
> they are all in league against me.
> God has left me at the mercy of malefactors
> and cast me into the clutches of evil men.
> I was at ease, but he set upon me and mauled me,
> seized me by the neck and worried me.
> He set me up as his target;
> his arrows rained upon me from every side;
> pitiless he cut deep into my vitals,
> he spilt my gall on the ground.
> He made breach after breach in my defences;
> he fell upon me like a fighting man.
> I stitched sackcloth together to cover my body
> and I buried my forelock in the dust;
> my cheeks were flushed with weeping
> and dark shadows were round my eyes
> yet my hands were free from violence
> and my prayer was sincere (16.9b–17; cf. 19.6–20).

Here there is no Satan upon whom to shift the blame, but only God, coldly and relentlessly hostile. Yet Job never doubts that this hostility can only rest on a horrible mistake. God must at very least be just, and Job remains convinced that if only he could present his case to God all would be well. But where and how?

> If only I knew how to find him,
> how to enter his court,
> I would state my case before him
> and set out my arguments in full;
> then I should learn what answer he would give
> and find out what he had to say.
> Would he exert his great power to browbeat me?
> No; God himself would never bring a charge against me.
> There the upright are vindicated before him,
> and I shall win from my judge an absolute discharge (23.3–9).

So, unlike Koheleth, Job must keep on hammering at what seems to be a closed door. Life must make sense – it doesn't; God must be just – he isn't. These disharmonies remain unresolved at the end of the dialogue with Job continuing to insist that his friends are offering him no more than the theological equivalent of meretricious 'muzak', incapable of reflecting or exploring the grim depths of human experience.

When we turn to the Psalms there is, as we have seen, abundant evidence for an attitude closer to that of Job's friends than to that of Job himself, an attitude which denies that there is any real problem of theodicy. Psalm 1 sketches out the contrast between the wicked/sinners/scornful (v.1) who are 'like chaff driven by the wind' (v.4), and the man whose life centres upon the torah of the Lord who is likened to a well-watered, evergreen, fruitful tree, 'in all that he does he prospers' (v.3). It ends by confidently affirming:

> The Lord knows (i.e. watches over) the way of the
> righteous, but the way of the wicked is doomed (v.6).

In Psalm 26 the psalmist protests his innocence in face of certain unspecified accusations, and confidently calls upon God to vindicate him on precisely the same grounds. He has hated the company of evildoers; he has not sat among the wicked (v.5). His life has been characterized by 'innocence' (v.6), by a delight in the worship of God (v.8), by 'integrity' (v.11). Therefore he looks forward to being the recipient of God's deliverance and favour, and to a time when his feet will be planted on firm ground (or among the upright). Then he will bless the Lord in the full assembly, the joyful gathering of God's worshipping community. Such confidence is expressed in its most dramatic form in Psalm 91 where the person who lives in the shadow of the Most High is assured:

> You shall not fear the hunter's trap by night
> or the arrow that flies by day,
> the pestilence that stalks in darkness
> or the plague raging at noonday.
> A thousand may fall at your side,
> ten thousand close at hand,
> but you it shall not touch;

his truth will be your shield and your rampart.
With your own eyes you shall see all this;
you shall watch the punishment of the wicked.
For you, the Lord is a safe retreat;
you have made the Most High your refuge.
No disaster shall befall you,
no calamity shall come upon your home (Ps. 91.5–10).

One can well imagine what Job's response would have been to that, and to many other Psalms which follow the same track.[22] Between him and such Psalms there is as wide a gulf as separates him from his friends. There are, however, other Psalms which probe more deeply because they are aware that life does not always conform to this script. Some Psalms draw attention to situations in which the wicked seem to be triumphing, while the righteous are perplexed. In Psalm 11 the psalmist, who has probably taken refuge in the temple, finds himself addressed by people who say to him:

Flee to the mountains like a bird;
see how the wicked string their bows
and fit the arrow to the string,
to shoot down honest men out of the darkness.
When foundations are undermined, what can the good
man do? (Ps. 11.1b–3)

Psalm 94 appeals to God to bring deserved punishment upon the arrogant, against the background of a situation in which they seem to be only too immune from such punishment:

How long shall the wicked, O Lord,
how long shall the wicked exult?
Evildoers are full of bluster,
boasting and swaggering;
they beat down thy people, O Lord,
and oppress thy chosen nation;
they murder the widow and the stranger
and do the fatherless to death;
they say, 'The Lord does not see,
the God of Jacob pays no heed' (Ps. 94.3–7).

Although this psalmist clings on to the belief that the triumph of the wicked is only temporary (v.13), he admits that he has had anxious or disquieting thoughts which express themselves in this and in many Psalms in questions directed to God (see chapter 4). Sometimes the anxiety spills over into vindictiveness against those whom the psalmist perceives to be his own, and God's enemies:

> May death strike them
> and may they perish in confusion,
> may they go down alive into Sheol;
> for their homes are haunts of evil (Ps. 55.14–15).

This theme is developed at length in Psalm 109.8ff. climaxing in the words:

> Curses he loved: may the curse fall on him!
> He took no pleasure in blessing: may no blessing be his!
> He clothed himself in cursing like a garment:
> may it seep into his body like water
>   and into his bones like oil!
> May it wrap him round like the clothes he puts on,
>   like the belt which he wears every day!
> May the Lord so requite my accusers
> and those who speak evil against me (Ps. 109.17–20).

Psalm 79 likewise calls for God's vengeance upon the heathen responsible for the destruction of the temple:

> Why should the nations ask, 'Where is their God?'
> Let thy vengeance for the bloody slaughter of thy servants
> fall on those nations before our very eyes.
> Let the groaning of the captives reach thy presence
> and in thy great might set free death's prisoners.
> As for the contempt our neighbours pour on thee, O Lord,
> turn it back sevenfold on their own heads.
> Then we thy people, the flock which thou dost shepherd,
> will give thee thanks for ever
> and repeat thy praise to every generation
>   (Ps. 79.10–13; cf. Ps. 137.7–9).

Anxiety, questioning, vindictiveness in the face of crises which seem to call into question people's belief in the power and justice of a God who in the past has displayed steadfast love towards his people (cf. Ps. 136). But how far do such anxiety and questioning go in the Psalms? Do they ever reach the point where faith itself seems to be under threat? Here Psalm 73 becomes central to the debate. It is a Psalm of contrasts and tensions, clearly marked out by certain recurring linguistic features within the Psalm. There is the tension between the 'indeeds' (Heb. *akh*) which introduce verse 1 and verse 13: 'God is *indeed* good to Israel, to the pure in heart'; these the opening words of the Psalm are echoed ironically by 'It is *indeed* in vain that I have kept my heart pure, and washed my hands in innocence' (v.13). So the question as to what kind of divine goodness this is is in the melting pot.

In between comes the account of the confusing and perplexing factors in life which make the psalmist green with envy – the wicked are doing very well, thank you (v.3); they are healthy and carefree, proud, popular, arrogantly influential and totally dismissive of God:

> 'What does God know?
> The Most High neither knows nor cares.'
> So wicked men talk, yet they still prosper,
> and rogues amass great wealth
> (vv.11–12).

Is God indeed good? Would it not be better to admit that seeking to follow in the ways of God is pointless, particularly since the psalmist's only reward is constant suffering and torment (v.14). Checked in the midst of this insidious doubt by the remembrance that he belongs to 'the generation of your children', the family of God, the believing community, the psalmist then goes on to describe the experience which is pivotal for the whole Psalm, 'I went into God's sacred courts' (v.17), literally, 'the holy places of God', which could also be interpreted with Buber as 'the holy mysteries of God'. Either way he is recounting an experience which has come to him in worship. And this leads immediately into the third '*indeed*', this time applied to the fate of the wicked: 'It is *indeed* on slippery ground that you have set them' (v.18). Their end is clear. In God's eyes they are no more substantial than images, shadows in a dream, shadows which disappear in the light of day:

cut off root and branch by death with all its terrors (v.19).

And with them is destroyed part of the reason for the psalmist's envy.

There is the four-fold repetition of the phrase 'and I' (Heb. *wa'ani*) in verses 2, 22, 23 and 28. The first 'And I' – my feet had almost stumbled – introduces the reason for the psalmist's perplexity and the threat to his faith. The other three 'and I's come on the other side of the psalmist's encounter with God in worship, two of them occurring in consecutive lines and describing different aspects of the psalmist's response to his experience. The first of them introduces a confession in which the psalmist acknowledges that his envy of the wicked had been rooted in one thing:

'And I' – I was a dolt. I did not understand,
> I was a mere beast as far as you were concerned,
>> O God (v.22).

The second introduces the positive response which made such envy wholly irrelevant:

'And I' – I am continually with you,
> you hold on to my right hand (v.23),

words that speak of God's revelation of himself to the psalmist not in words, but as Buber has it, through a gesture, '. . . as in the dark a father takes his little son by the hand, certainly to lead him, but primarily in order to make present to him, in the warm touch of coursing blood, the fact that he, the father, is continually with him.'[23] The final 'And I' introduces the last verse of the Psalm, and indicates how the perspective within the Psalm has changed. No longer is it a contrast between 'the pure in heart' and the wicked; the contrast is now between 'those who are far from you who perish' (v.27) 'and I' who now know that my 'good' consists in being near to God (v.28).

It is not difficult to see a certain kinship between Psalm 73 and the book of Job. Both are struggling to come to terms with a powerful contradiction which lies close to the heart of the problem of theodicy, the contradiction between talk of the goodness of God and the bitter fact that in this God's world the godless wicked all too often flourish, while the servants of God

experience pain and suffering. Neither Psalm 73 nor the book of
Job provide a coherent, rational answer – nor does any other part
of the Old Testament as far as I am aware.[24] But both take the
contradiction seriously and refuse to hide behind widely accepted answers. This leads the psalmist to the point of questioning whether it makes any sense to go on believing in the goodness
of God; it drives Job to hurl angry and accusing questions at God
and to deplore God's aloofness and indifference to his plight. In
neither case is the contradiction resolved on an intellectual level.
Both, however, discover that 'the man who struggles for God is
near Him, even when he imagines he is driven far from God.[25]
Both of them find their peace in a moment of revelation. The
counterpart to the psalmist's:

> I am continually with you,
> you hold on to my right hand (Ps. 73.23)

is to be found in Job's final response to the God of mystery and
power who questions him:

> I know that you can do all things
> and that no purpose is beyond you.
> But I have spoken of great things I have not understood,
> things too wonderful for me to know.
> Once I knew of you only by report,
> but now I see you with my own eyes   (Job 42.2–3).

There is, however, a difference, an important difference. The
God who comes to Job is the God who answers him out of the
whirlwind, a God of awesome majesty and power, a God who
crushes Job into accepting that he has no right to continue to
argue with such a God, a God who overpowers Job with a torrent
of words. Certainly, as Eichrodt avers, there is no way in which
you can place this God 'on the same level as the world' or make
him into 'an object of knowledge'.[26] But is there any way of
getting him out of the whirlwind? Job may see this God with his
own eyes, but isn't this a seeing from a distance? It is the
psalmist's experience that in worship this distance is overcome:

> I am continually with you,
> you hold on to my right hand (v.23).
>
> For me it is good to be near God (v.28).

The greatest of all the poets of theodicy remains in the end a poet, depicting in unsurpassed imagery a universe too complicated for man to understand and a God too mysterious to be the object of man's scrutiny. This emphasis upon the mystery and the transcendence of God is an essential element in Israel's faith – and, I believe, in any faith. It is an element which is celebrated over and over again in hymns of praise in the Psalter (e.g. Pss. 145, 148). But in itself if is not enough. The mystery must become tangible, the transcendent must draw near, and it is to this, as it happens in worship, that the psalmist bears witness.

Chapter 6

The Problem of Death

The danger of making sweeping generalizations in the field of religious beliefs is nowhere greater than in the realm of people's attitude to death. Here it is possible for logically inconsistent patterns of belief to lie comfortably side by side, not only within a culture, but within an individual's thinking. Any analysis of attitudes towards death and life hereafter within the Christian church at the present day would soon reveal a curious blend of New Testament resurrection concepts, Platonic ideas concerning the immortality of the soul, and a touch of spiritualism. How much greater then are the dangers in attempting to generalize about attitudes towards death in cultures and religions from which we are separated not only by historical but by ideological barriers.[1]

When we turn to consider the two major civilizations with which Israel's wisdom teachers and writers had certain affinities, an immediate contrast becomes apparent. We have already had occasion to note the importance of the mortuary cults in Egyptian life and thought. Their prevalence is to be seen against the background of a dominant conviction put thus by an Egyptologist: 'We can safely say that the Egyptians of the historical period always believed in immortality, though there is no word for immortality in their language. The same word "life" is used for earthly existence and for existence after death.'[2] If in the earliest period immortality was posited only for the king, by the end of the Old Kingdom, i.e. well before 2000 BCE, it had been thoroughly democratized. That does not mean that there is in Egyptian thought any agreed picture of what happened to human beings after death. There was a variety of ideologies: for example, the dead ascended to the sky to continue their existence as stars, or they joined Osiris to share in his rule of the underworld, or they accompanied the sun-god Re as he journeyed in his barque across the sky, or in the tombs the dead extended their earthly life, enjoying to the full all they had attained in this present life.

One thing, however, is clear whatever the ideology: 'The Egyptians . . . considered death as an interruption, not the end of life – a change in man's personality, not its annihilation.'[3] If we ask why such a belief should have been so powerful in ancient Egypt, various theories come into play. In the context of the worship of the sun-god Re, for example, it has been argued that: 'When the sunset is inseparable from the thought of death, the dawn is a surety of resurrection. The relevance of the natural phenomena to human problems is a matter of direct experience, not of intellectual argument. It is an intuitive insight, not a theory. It induces faith, not knowledge.'[4] The distinctions in this statement between 'intuitive insight' and 'theory', 'faith' and 'knowledge' smack very much of modern Western assumptions, which may not be applicable to ancient Egyptian thought. Such life beyond the present, usually located in the West where the sun sets, is often depicted as a place of quietude and happiness. A fourteenth-century text carved on the walls of a tomb at Thebes, after decrying contemporary songs which seek to denigrate the land of eternity in the interests of magnifying life here and now, describes this land of eternity as:

> The right and the true, without terrors.
> Quarrelling is its abomination,
> And there is no one who arrays himself against his
>   fellow.
> This land which has no opponent –
> All our kinsfolk rest in it since the first day of
>   time.
> They who are to be, for millions of millions,
> Will all have come to it.
> There exists none who may tarry in the land of Egypt;
> There is not one who fails to reach yon place.
> As for the duration of what is done on earth,

It is a kind of dream;
(But) they say: 'Welcome, safe and sound!'
To him who reaches the West.[5]

The more we become aware of cultural and religious contacts between Ancient Egypt and Israel, the more similarities are traced between Old Testament proverbial material and Egyptian Instruction literature,[6] the more linguistic and thematic links are found between Egyptian hymns and some of the Psalms, the more interesting it becomes that this central element in Egyptian thought seems to be conspicuous by its absence in Hebrew wisdom literature and in most of the Psalms.

To turn from Egypt to Mesopotamia, whether in Sumerian literature or in later Babylonian texts which often retell and reshape earlier material, is to enter a different world, a world in which 'death was accepted in a truly matter of fact way',[7] and what lay beyond death had little to offer of either hope or attractiveness. As S. N. Kramer puts it, on death man 'went to the world below, never to return. Needless to say this was a source of anxiety and perplexity: the problem of death and the nether world was beset with enigmas, paradoxes and dilemmas, and it is no wonder that Sumerian ideas pertaining to them were neither precise nor consistent.'[8] This nether world seems to have been viewed as a hugh cosmic space below the earth. Entrance to it was normally by the grave. It had its own fiercesome and unattractive deities, Ereshkigal and Nergal, its own rules and regulations. It was a world of little hope or joy, even for the good and the deserving, a world in which life was no more than 'a dismal, wretched reflection of life on earth.'[9] All the connotations associated with this world are chill, depressing and negative. Some Sumerian texts suggest that the sun, after setting, continues its journey through this nether world at night, just as the moon spends the last day of the month, his 'day of sleep', there. Night and darkness, but never as in Egyptian thought the corresponding image of dawn as the surety of resurrection and new life. That there are strong affinities between this Sumerian netherworld called Kur and the biblical concept of Sheol will become apparent.

Death, with subsequent descent to this chill underworld, seems to have raised no theological problems for the Sumerians. This was the pattern of creation. The gods had been created first and were by definition immortal. Man was then created to be the servant of the gods, to ensure that the gods were properly honoured and housed. Once man's brief allotted span of life was over and he had done his duty to the gods, the nether world awaited him, a world in which there was neither bliss nor reward. This was the generally accepted premiss of Babylonian thought. You didn't need to be a pessimist to accept that:

> (Whatever) men do does not last for ever.
> Mankind and their achievements alike come to an end.[10]

But there is evidence in Babylonian texts that the premiss was not accepted unquestioningly. If the gods live for ever, why should not man likewise live for ever? Two famous Babylonian texts touch on this issue. In the one, Adapa, protege of Ea, god of wisdom, patron god of exorcists, is in trouble. In a fit of temper he has broken the wing of the south wind which capsized his boat one day when he was out fishing. He is summoned to appear before the sky-god Anu. Ea advises him to go suitably penitent, hair dishevelled and dressed as a mourner, and warns him not to accept any hospitality since what he is going to be offered is 'the bread of death' and 'the water of death'. Adapa follows this advice to the letter. When there is placed before him what is in fact 'the bread of life', he refuses to eat; when he is offered what is in fact 'the water of life' he refuses to drink. Anu, amused at this strange conduct, turns to him and says:

> Come now, Adapa! Why didst thou neither eat nor drink?
> Thou shalt not have (eternal) life . . .

When Adapa tries to excuse his conduct by saying he was simply following Ea's advice, Anu retorts: 'Take him away and return him to this earth.'[11] Back home at Eridu Adapa may be the wisest of men, blameless, the most scrupulous devotee of the gods, but eternal life he does not have. There are certain puzzling features in this story. It is not clear, for example, what Ea's motives were in warning Adapa not to accept hospitality from Anu. Was he suspicious that Anu might be up to some skulduggery or was he deliberately trying to make sure that Adapa would not become immortal by sharing in the good of the gods? One thing, however, is clear. The boundary line between the gods and man, even the wisest and best of men, remains firmly drawn. The gods enjoy eternal life, men don't. It is not Adapa's fault that he does not obtain eternal life. He is the innocent victim. The gods themselves ensure that he does not obtain immortality.

The other text is the longest and perhaps the most famous of all Babylonian texts, the Epic of Gilgamesh. Gilgamesh's boon companion Enkidu is involved in many a hair-raising escapade, some of which give offence to the gods. Distraught by the death of Enkidu, and dreading a like fate, Gilgamesh sets out to consult Utnapishtim, survivor of the flood which had wiped out the rest of the human race, the Mesopotamian Noah who now lives in the far distant island of the blessed. On the day he is warned by lady Siduri, the inn keeper, to accept the inevitability of death:

> Gilgamesh, where are you rushing?
> The life which you seek you will not find,
> For when the gods created mankind
> They assigned death to men,
> But held life in their keeping.
> As for yourself, Gilgamesh, fill your belly,
> Day and night be happy,
> Every day have pleasure,
> Day and night dance and rejoice,
> Put on clean clothes,
> Wash your head, bathe in water,
> Gaze on the little one who holds your hand
> Let your spouse be happy in your bosom.[12]

But Gilgamesh persists in his futile search. When he eventually reaches Utnapishtim, Utnapishtim underlines to him the same message of the transitoriness and frailty of human life. To emphasize the impossibility of achieving immortality he challenges Gilgamesh to stay awake for six days and seven nights. After being convinced that he had failed the test – he quickly dozes off – Gilgamesh acknowledges that:

> The Snatcher has hold of my flesh,
> Death sits in my bedchamber,
> And wherever I set my feet, there is death.[13]

As Gilgamesh prepares to return home Utnapishtim reveals to him the secret whereabouts of a plant called 'Man becomes young in old age'. Having obtained the plant Gilgamesh begins his homeward journey only to stop after a tiring day's travel beside a pool of cool water. While he bathes in the water:

> A serpent sniffed the fragrance of the plant;
> It came up (from the water) and carried off the plant.
> Going back it shed its slough.[14]

Thus the plant which could for ever renew his life is gone. It is the snake that is perpetually rejuvenated as it periodically casts off its old skin. All that remains is for Gilgamesh to return home to Erech, there to seek consolation in the greatness and the beauty of the city he rules, until the time comes when he too will be summoned to that nether world from which there is no return. The optimism of ancient Egypt in the face of death finds its counterpart in Mesopotamian pessimism; the 'Welcome, safe and sound! To him who reaches the West' becomes 'Gilgamesh, where are you rushing? The life which you seek you will not find.' Death remains, part of the definition of what it means to be human.

On the whole it is this Mesopotamian ethos surrounding death which is characteristic of both the wisdom literature and the Psalms in the Old Testament. Since the book of Proverbs is concerned primarily with commending attitudes and ways of conduct which lead to successful living, and issuing warnings against attitudes and ways of conduct which lead to trouble and disaster, it is hardly surprising that there is little about death in Proverbs. What there is, is concerned in the main with stressing the dire consequences of certain foolish actions. Thus among the things from which wisdom delivers her devotees is involvement with the 'strange' or 'foreign' woman:[15]

> For her house sinks down to death,
> and her paths to the shades;
> none who go to her come back,
> nor do they regain the paths of life (Prov. 2. 18–19).

> Many a victim has she laid low;
> all her slain are a mighty host.
> Her house is the way to Sheol,
> going down to the chambers of death (Prov. 7. 26–7; cf. 5.5).

Anyone who foolishly yields to her seductive advances:

> Does not know that the shades are there,
> that her guests are in the depths of Sheol (Prov. 9.18).

In such passages we meet with what is typical in the Old Testament, the thought of death as a going down to Sheol, a place inhabited by the shades (Heb. *rephaim*); cf. Job 26.5; Ps. 88.11; Isa. 26.19.

To hate wisdom is to be 'in love with death' (Prov. 8.36). *Per contra* it is wisdom and the teaching of the wise that point the way to life:

> The teaching of the wise is the fountain of life,
> that one may avoid the snares of death (Prov. 13.14).

The same statement reappears in 14.27 with 'the fear of the Lord' taking the place of 'the teaching of the wise'. In a series of contrasting statements in chapter 11 we find:

> Riches do not profit in the day of wrath,
> but righteousness delivers from death.

> When the wicked dies his hope perishes,
> and the expectation of the godless comes to naught.

> He who is steadfast in righteousness will live,
> but he who pursues evil will die (Prov. 11. 4, 7, 19).

It would be quite wrong to assume from such statements that Proverbs is saying that a) it is only the wicked who die, and b) the righteous have hope in a life that transcends death. Such proverbial sayings are moving strictly within the confines of this world. They are drawing a contrast between the righteous who may expect to enjoy a long and full life, and the wicked whose conduct leads to premature death. But at the end there awaits both, the righteous and the wicked, Sheol, like an insatiable monster whose appetite is never satisfied:[16]

> Three things are never satisfied;
> four things never say 'Enough':
> Sheol, the barren womb,
> the earth ever thirsty for water
> and the fire which never says 'Enough' (Prov. 30.15b–16).

The picture of Sheol, with its associated terms such as the Pit (Heb. *shahath*) and Destruction (Heb. *abaddon*) is graphically filled out by several passages in the book of Job. In chapter 7 Job complains about his present brief pain-filled life, soon to come to an end:

> As clouds break up and disperse,
> so he that goes down to Sheol never comes back;
> he never returns home again,
> and his place will know him no more (7.9–10).

Although the word Sheol does not occur the dark negativity for which it stands is nowhere more vividly described than in 10.20–22, where Job protests to God:

> Is not my life short and fleeting?
> Let me be, that I may be happy for a moment,
> before I depart to a land of gloom,
> a land of deep darkness, never to return,
> a land of gathering shadows,
> of deepening darkness, lit by no ray of light,
> dark upon dark.

This dark world from which there is no return is a world devoid of all that makes life meaningful:

> If I measure Sheol for my house,
> if I spread my couch in the darkness,
> if I call the grave my father
> and the worm my mother or my sister,
> where, then, will my hope be,
> or who will take account of my piety?
> I cannot take them down to Sheol with me,
> nor can they descend with me into the earth (17.13–16).

There are no rewards and no judgment in Sheol. It is part of Job's bitter refutation of his friends that not only do the wicked enjoy long life and success in this world, but:

> Their lives close in prosperity,
> and they go down to Sheol in peace (21.13).

In some respects the Hebrew picture of Sheol is much more bleak and negative than the Babylonian. At least in Babylonian thought the underworld had its own deities, fiercesome and implacable maybe, but operating their own rules and regulations. Hebrew faith evacuated Sheol of such deities. It remains a place of unconsciousness as opposed to the vitality of this world.

The chill negativity, the bleak destructiveness of this concept of death is at its most notable in the book of Ecclesiastes. Like a true wisdom teacher Koheleth makes out a case for believing that it is preferable to be a wise man rather than to be a fool, but in the end the same fate overtakes them both: 'Alas, wise man and fool die the same death' (2.16). This translation assumes an attitude of resignation in the face of death. There is, however, much to be said for hearing in these words the voice of protest – why should a wise man die just like a fool?[17] Yet the fact cannot be questioned, as Koheleth echoing the language and imagery of Genesis 2–3 puts it: 'For man is a creature of chance and the beasts are creatures of chance, and one mischance awaits them all: death comes to both alike. They all draw the same breath. Men have no advantage over beasts; for everything is emptiness. All go to the same place: all came from the dust, and to the dust all return. Who knows whether the spirit (or life) of man goes upward or whether the spirit (or life) of the beast goes downward to the earth' (Eccles. 3.19–21). In face of speculation that there may possibly be something other for man after death than Sheol, Koheleth simply shrugs his shoulders and says 'who knows?'. Life has its problems and its perplexities, but to be alive is still to have hope. Remember, he says, 'a live dog is better than a dead lion. True, the living know that they will die; but the dead know nothing. There are no more rewards for them: they are utterly forgotten. For them, love, hate, ambition, all are now over' (9.4–6). Koheleth's last words are a haunting poem contrasting the vigour of youth with the debilitating effects of old age (12.1–9). The images in this poem, rich and subtle, are capable of a variety of interpretations,[18] but they all point forward to the one certainty: 'For man goes to his everlasting home, and the mourners go about the streets. Remember him (i.e. God) before the silver cord is snapped and the golden bowl is broken, before the pitcher is shattered at the spring and the wheel broken at the well, before the dust returns to the earth as it began and the spirit returns to God who gave it. Emptiness, emptiness, says Koheleth, all is empty' (12.5b–8). In his attitude towards death

Koheleth is saying no more than other and earlier wisdom teachers, yet one senses behind his words an emotional protest. Having banished God to the remotest heaven, he has no foundation upon which to build anything else.

When we turn to the Psalms the same chill image of Sheol and death abounds, but with this difference. Since worship focusses upon the reality of the believer's relationship with the living God, it is the end of that relationship which to many psalmists is the most destructive and perplexing feature of death. Thus in Psalm 6, the psalmist in his plea to God to deliver him from pressing troubles, reminds God – or complains or protests to God – that:

> In death there is no remembrance of you;
> in Sheol who can give you praise? (Ps. 6.5; cf. 115.17)

In Psalm 30, a Psalm of thanksgiving for recovery from serious illness, the psalmist recalls that part of his plea to God lay in certain unanswerable questions:

> What profit is there in my death, if I go down to the Pit?
> Will the dust praise you? will it tell of your
>   faithfulness?   (30.9; cf. Hezekiah's prayer,
>   Isa. 38. 18–19)

In a moment of darkest crisis the psalmist in Psalm 88 reaches out to God:

> Every day I call upon you, O Lord;
> I spread out my hands to you.
> Do you work wonders for the dead?
> Do the shades rise up to praise you?
> Is your steadfast love declared in the grave,
> or your faithfulness in Abaddon?
> Are your wonders known in the darkness
> or your saving power in the land of forgetfulness?
>   (88.9–12)

And the expected answer to all these questions is 'No'.

The language of death and Sheol, however, serves another function, particularly in the Psalms. Return for a moment to Psalm 30. In verse 3 the psalmist describes what God has done for him in the following terms:

O Lord, you have brought me up from Sheol,
you have restored me to life from among those who go
down to the Pit.

Sheol, the Pit, death are regarded as present realities whenever people are caught up in a life-threatening situation, whether it be for example serious illness, betrayal by friends, false accusations by enemies or oppression by the powerful. Death is thus regarded as the negative aspect of life, or as A. R. Johnson put it: '. . . death is to be explained in terms of life. It is a weak, and indeed, in so far as it marks the final disintegration of one's *nephesh*, the weakest form of life . . . , man is further depicted as living on, a mere shadow of his former self in company of the *rephaim* in the underworld of Sheol.'[19] Death and life are, therefore, not regarded as absolute opposites. Death and the power of death, Sheol and its tentacles, are present in the midst of life, wherever the fulness of life is under attack. Thus a situation of dire crisis in life can be described as follows:

The cords of death encompassed me,
the torrents of perdition assailed me;
the cords of Sheol entangled me,
the snares of death confronted me (Ps. 18.4–5; cf.116.3).

And in Psalm 88:

. . . my soul is full of troubles,
and my life draws near to Sheol.
I am reckoned among those who go down to the Pit;
I am a man who has no strength,
like one forsaken among the dead,
like the slain that lie in the grave,
like those whom you remember no more,
for they are cut off from your hand.
You have put me in the depths of the Pit,
in regions dark and deep (vv. 3–6).

When, therefore, a psalmist talks about God delivering him from death (56.13) or from the depths of Sheol (86.13) or lifting him up from the gates of death (9.13) he is normally talking about experiences of deliverance from life-threatening situations in this world, not about any ultimate deliverance from death or any hope of meaningful life beyond this present life. But is this always the case? Psalm 49 is a Psalm which has more than its fair share of critical problems, both as to its text and its *Sitz im Leben*. It is usually classified as a 'wisdom psalm'. Perdue regarded it as 'a didactic poem written within the context of a school or even within the milieu of the court, since the wealthy and "the men of the world" (diplomats) are among the audience'.[20] E. Gerstenberger, *per contra*, treats it as a synagogial meditation and instruction. 'A cantor, perhaps a professional and perhaps the leader of his religious group, presents the Psalm to the congregation . . . in order to teach the hearers endurance and hope in a rather miserable situation of economic and political dependency.'[21] 'Perhaps' is the operative word on many such verdicts. The affinities of the Psalm with the wisdom tradition can hardly be doubted, however they be explained. The introduction (vv.1–3) addresses 'all the inhabitants of the earth', not simply Israel, and it claims to be concerned with 'wisdom' and 'understanding', 'proverb' and 'riddle'. The central theme of the Psalm is to be found in a refrain which occurs twice, in verse 12 and verse 20:

> Man cannot abide in his pomp,
> he is like the beasts that perish (cf. Eccles. 3.19).

Most English translations, even those which like the NEB alter the text, treat verses 12 and 20 as if they were the same text. The Hebrew, however, in verse 20 reads:

> Man in his pomp – and he does not understand,
> he is like the beasts that perish.

The variation may be correct and deliberate. It is human failure to understand the frailty and transitoriness of life which is a central theme of the Psalm, in particular the failure at this point of the rich and the powerful. The Psalm argues that money can ensure many things, but not a permanent lease of life. Using the language of paying a ransom, the Psalm insists that:

> . . no man can ever ransom himself
> nor pay God the price of that release;
> his ransom would cost too much,
> for ever beyond his power to pay,

> the ransom that would let him live on always,
> and never see the Pit (vv.7–9).

Wise and fool alike go to their eternal home (cf. Eccles. 3.19) and from this fate not even the most brazenly self-confident are exempt:

> Like sheep they are appointed for Sheol;
> Death shall be their shepherd;
> straight to the grave they descend,
> and their form shall waste away;
> Sheol shall be their home.
> (v.14; cf. vv.17–19 and Ps. 73.18–20)[22]

Over against this, the psalmist who in all probability belongs to the poor and the oppressed, states his confidence in the words:

> But God will ransom my soul from the power of Sheol,
> for he will receive me (v.15).

What does this mean? Is it laying claim to some hope in a life that transcends death, or is it more modest? Very similar language is found in Elihu's speech in Job 33, a speech in which he is presenting his case against what he can only regard as Job's arrogant defiance of God and his blind failure to see how God deals with men. In spite of what Job has been arguing, Elihu claims that God does speak to men. He speaks through dreams (vv.15–18), he speaks through suffering (vv.19–22) and he speaks through healing (vv.23–28). In the earlier dialogue with his friends Job had expressed the hope that there would come forward a witness who would speak for him in heaven (cf. 16.18ff.), rather in the way in which a personal deity would present a sufferer's case to the other gods in Babylonian thought. Here Elihu introduces in verse 23 the figure of a mediator (Heb. *melis*) or advocate for the defence – the opposite of the *satan* in the prologue – one who will be gracious to the defendant and say:

> Deliver him from going down to the Pit,
> I have found a ransom (Job 33.24).

There is no indication as to what that ransom is, but its effect is clear – healing, a 'return to the days of his youthful vigour' (v.25), restoration to God's presence, a sense of joy and forgiveness, the threat of death withdrawn:

> He has redeemed my soul from going down to the Pit,
> and my life shall see the light (v.28),

striking contrast to the closing comment on the rich in Psalm 49.19:

> He will go to join the company of his forefathers,
> who will never again see the light.

Job 33, therefore, in using the language of 'ransom' and 'redeeming . . . from going down to Sheol' is talking about a hoped-for renewal of vitality in this life, for someone suffering from a debilitating illness. There is no suggestion in this language in Job 33 of any hope in life beyond death. There is, therefore, a strong case for arguing that Psalm 49.15 ought to be interpreted along the same lines, i.e. that the psalmist is expressing his conviction that he will be delivered by God from the rich and arrogant persecutors whose actions have blighted and darkened his life, and thus once again experience life in all its fulness. Or is there more to be said? Do the words of Ps. 49.15 point, as many commentators suggest,[23] to a man reaching out towards a lasting fellowship with God which he is convinced not even death can destroy? Much here depends on the interpretation we give to the apparently simple words 'for he will receive me'. The Hebrew verb translated 'received' (*lkh*) is the verb which is used in the strange statement about Enoch in Gen.5.24, 'Enoch walked with God; and he was not, for God *took* him'. It also occurs twice in the narrative of Elijah's final mysterious disappearance heavenwards in the whirlwind in II Kings 2.9, 10. In both cases later tradition saw in these statements a reference to someone who had side-stepped or conquered death. Thus Hebrews 11.5, 'By faith Enoch was taken up so that he should not see death; and he was not found because God had taken him.' The only other occurrence in the Psalms of God 'receiving' or taking a person is in Psalm 73 where the psalmist, after expressing his confidence that he is continually with God, being held and guided, adds 'and afterwards you will receive me to glory (or honour)' (Ps. 73.24). These words have provoked endless discussion, and to say as one recent commentator has 'The meaning is evident enough; the psalmist finds the solution to the inconsistencies of life in the final reward of the righteous after death',[24] seems to me suspiciously like whistling in the dark. The syntax of this statement is difficult, and it is not clear what is meant by either 'glory' or 'afterwards'. Broadly speaking there are two lines of interpretation: (1) the words refer to the psalmist's belief that after his experience of pain, suffering and doubt, he will be restored in this life to his proper place of honour and acceptance in the community: and (2) the words 'afterwards' and 'glory' are pointing to something beyond this present life, to a hope which transcends death. Which is more likely? Or are there perhaps elements of both in these words? Certainly the depth and reality of the psalmist's worship-mediated conviction that he is *continually* with God lies, as we have seen,[25] at the heart of everything that Psalm 73 has to say. Does this then justify Calvin's comment, 'kabod/glory in my opinion ought not to be confined to eternal life, as some do; but it embraces the whole range of our happiness, from a beginning which is experienced now on earth, to the end for which we hope in heaven'?[26] The text seems to me to be too ambiguous for any solid case to be built upon it. If this is true of Ps. 73.24 and Ps. 49.15, how much more must it be true of that other passage from the book of Job which the RSV with considerable and commendable diffidence translates:

> For I know that my Redeemer (or Vindicator) lives,
> and at last he will stand upon the earth;
> and after my skin has been thus destroyed,
> then from my flesh (or without my flesh) I shall see God,
> whom I shall see on my side,
> and my eyes shall behold, and not another
>
> (Job 19.25–27).[27]

From context it is clear that these words express Job's passionate and unshakable conviction that one day he will be vindicated. But who is this 'Redeemer' (Heb. *goel* kinsman)? Is he merely a kinsman of Job who will survive him one day to witness his rehabilitation in the eyes of the community, or is he God, or is he some angelic mediator or defending counsel? And when is such vindication to take place – before death 'from my flesh' or after death 'without my flesh'? There is no use pretending to certainty on these matters. None is to be had.

We must accept that, on the whole, the Psalms and the wisdom literature share an approach to death which regards death as the final disintegration of all meaningful life, and a descent into the darkness and bleakness of Sheol. For the wisdom writers this seems to pose no theological problems. For many of the psalmists the darkness and bleakness of Sheol contain an added menace since to be in Sheol means to be cut off from the God who comes to them in worship.[28] Yet this fact by no means destroyed or weakened their faith in a God of steadfast love. Earlier we indicated that in face of death Koheleth could make no more than an emotional response since he had banished God to the remotest heaven. This could never be the psalmists' response, since they believed in the nearness and in the saving presence of God. There is one Psalm which daringly questions whether this could not be the worshipper's experience even in and after death. Haunted by a sense of the inescapable presence of God in every situation in life, he asks:

> Whither shall I go from your Spirit?
> Or whither shall I flee from your presence?
> If I ascend to heaven, you are there!
> If I make my bed in Sheol, you are there!
> If I take the wings of the morning
> and dwell in the uttermost parts of the sea,
> even there your hand shall lead me,
> and your right hand shall hold me.
> If I say, 'Let only darkness cover me,
> and the light about me be night,'
> even the darkness is not dark to you,
> the night is as bright as the day;
> for darkness is as light with you (Ps. 139.7–12).

God is there . . . in Sheol – a simple statement, a leap of faith devoid of any theorizing or elaboration; yet no more is needed to suggest an approach to death which will ultimately take us far beyond the bounds of either Israel's wisdom literature or much of Israel's experience in worship.

Chapter 7

Wisdom and Worship – The Contribution of Jesus ben Sirach

Shortly after 132 BCE the grandson of Jesus ben Sirach of Jerusalem translated his grandfather's 'Wisdom' into Greek for the benefit of those 'who have made their home in a foreign land, and wish to become scholars by training themselves to live according to the law' (Prologue). He did so with a certain diffidence, recognizing that 'it is impossible for a translator to find precise equivalents for the original Hebrew in another language'. He would no doubt have been doubly cautious of an interpretation of his grandfather's wisdom which depends to some extent on a translation of a translation – although significant sections of the Hebrew text of Sirach are now available to us.[1] Sirach, who probably wrote round about 180 BCE, was a well-travelled man of the world, a professional wisdom teacher who invited pupils to enrol in his school. The tuition fees seem to have been fairly hefty; but Sirach was in no doubt that his pupils, if they applied themselves to the discipline of study, would receive value for money:

> Your share of instruction may cost you a large sum of silver,
> but it will bring you a large return in gold (51.28).

In many respects the Wisdom of Sirach stands in the tradition of the book of Proverbs. It has certain of the formal characteristics of proverbial teaching – for example, the address to the pupil as 'my son' (2.1; 4,1; 6.18, etc.), numerical sayings (37.18), illustrations drawn from the world of nature (11.3,30; 12.13, etc.). It is packed with shrewd observation and comment upon a wide variety of social and ethical topics long handled by wisdom teachers – family life, the problems of being tied to an unsatisfactory wife (25.13–26; 26.5–12), the joys of a good wife (26.1–4, 13–18; 36.21–26), the worries of having a daughter (42.9–14) – a passage which ends in the not unprejudiced remark:

> Better a man's wickedness than a woman's goodness;
> it is a woman who brings shame and disgrace.

Attention is drawn to the need to discipline a son (30.1–13) and the importance of knowing and abiding by the social graces (31.12–32.13). Warnings are given against gluttony (37.27–31), and sexual promiscuity (23.16–27). Repeatedly advice is offered about the damage that can be inflicted by 'the tongue' (5.10–14; 23.7–15, etc.), and the destructive potential of anger (27.30–28.7). There is the plea for compassion towards the poor, the widow and the orphan (4.1–10). The value of a sound education is underlined (6.32–37) – and much else. It has often been noted, however, that Sirach differs from his predecessors in Israel's wisdom tradition because of his interest in integrating Israel's wider religious heritage into his wisdom thought. Thus while earlier wisdom books such as Proverbs, Job and Ecclesiastes, have little or nothing to say about the historical dimension of Israel's religious traditions, Sirach in a long section from chapters 44–49 produces his roll-call of the heroes of Israel's past and surveys their activities in the same order as they now lie before us in the Hebrew Bible, beginning with Enoch on through the patriarchs, Moses and the exodus and wilderness themes, the former prophets and kings, to the major prophetic figures of Isaiah, Jeremiah and Ezekiel. All this is consistent with the extent to which Sirach repeatedly draws upon earlier scriptural material, not merely the wisdom books but also Genesis 1–11, the patriarchal traditions, Deutero–Isaiah and the Psalms.[2] As has been correctly pointed out: 'The wise man can equally appeal to the experience of the intelligent man and to the sacred writings. Of this method Jesus ben Sirach is a model.'[3] Furthermore in Sirach 'Wisdom' has been thoroughly integrated into mainstream Jewish religious thought of the post-exilic period. Not only does the book begin with the words:

> All wisdom is from the Lord;
> wisdom is with him for ever (1.1),

but wisdom is identified with 'torah', the law. In the eulogy of wisdom in chapter 24 – which has its roots in the speech of personified wisdom in Proverbs 8.22–9.6, but which as we shall see goes significantly beyond it – all that wisdom is and all that she has to offer is not only at home in Israel, but more specifically it is claimed:

> All this is the covenant-book of God Most High,
> the law which Moses enacted to be the heritage of the
> assemblies of Jacob (24.23).

We have been arguing in previous chapters that there is a much closer relationship between wisdom and worship in Israel than is sometimes recognized, and that if, in von Rad's words, in Sirach 'the teacher has become a worshipper' he may not have been the first to do so. It is now time, however, to take a closer look at the way in which wisdom and worship are integrated in the thought of Sirach.

In commending his credentials as a wisdom teacher, Sirach, in the epilogue of the book, says:

> When I was still young, before I set out on my travels,
> I asked openly for wisdom in my prayers.
> In the forecourt of the sanctuary I laid claim to her,
> and I shall seek her out to the end (51.13).

Likewise in his description of the craft of the wisdom teacher in 39.1–11, he points to a man who studies 'the law of the Most High', who investigates the wisdom of the past, who:

> . . . preserves the sayings of famous men
> and penetrates the intricacies of parables.
> He investigates the hidden meaning of proverbs
> and knows his way among riddles (39.2–3).

A man who travels extensively to investigate the human condition at first hand, but also a man who:

> . . . makes a point of rising early
> to pray to the Lord, his Makèr,
> and prays aloud to the Most High,
> asking pardon for his sins (39.5).

That this is no formal nod to what is regarded as religiously respectable becomes clear in several key features of the book.

1. In his survey of the heroes of Israel's past in chapters 44–49 he includes a wide variety of people who contributed in different ways to the life of Israel:

> Some held sway over kingdoms
> and made themselves a name by their exploits.
> Others were sage counsellors,
> who spoke out with prophetic power.
> Some led the people by their counsels
> and by their knowledge of the nation's law;
> out of their fund of wisdom they gave instruction.
> Some were composers of music or writers of poetry.
> Others were endowed with wealth and strength,
> living peacefully in their homes (44.3–6).

If the distribution of the material is anything to go by, however, pride of place is given to those who are associated with Israel's tradition of worship. Thus while Moses is commended in five verses (45.1–5), brother Aaron with whom God 'made a perpetual covenant . . . conferring on him the priesthood of the nation' (45.7) is allotted seventeen verses (45.6–22), verses which lovingly describe his priestly vestments, his dual function in terms of sacrifice and a teaching ministry, and his special place within the community. It is in keeping with this that the historical survey ends with a glowing eulogy of Simon, son of Onias, high priest in Jerusalem towards the end of the third century and the beginning of the second century BCE:

> in whose lifetime the house was repaired,
> in whose days the temple was fortified (50.1).

He depicts Simon leading the people in worship, standing by the altar surrounded by the sons of Aaron:

> . . . like a young cedar of Lebanon
> in the midst of a circle of palms (50.12),

pronouncing upon the people the priestly blessing (Num. 6.24–26) on the day of atonement. In the light of this Sirach himself summons people to worship:

> Come then, praise the God of the universe,
> who everywhere works great wonders,
> who from our birth enables our life
> and deals with us in mercy.
> May he grant us a joyful heart,
> and in our time send Israel lasting peace.
> May he confirm his mercy towards us,
> and in his own good time grant us deliverance (50.22–24).

2. The book of Sirach is also noteworthy for the way in which we find, incorporated within a wisdom framework, didactic poems celebrating the greatness of God, hymns and prayers. Thus the section 16.24–17.14 begins with a formal wisdom type introduction:

> Listen to me, my son, and learn sense;
> pay close attention to what I say;
> I will show you exact discipline
> and teach you accurate knowledge (16.24–25).

It then moves into a long poem celebrating the works of the Lord, the ordered universe and in particular his creation of man, a poem which draws extensively upon the creation hymn in Genesis 1 and Psalms such as Psalms 8 and 144. The section on the craft of the wisdom teacher in 39.1–11 (see above) is immediately followed by a lyrical poem introduced by the words:

> I have still more in my mind to express;
> I am full like the moon at mid-month.
> Listen to me, my devout sons, and blossom
> like a rose planted by a stream.
> Spread your fragrance like incense
> and bloom like a lily.
> Scatter your fragrance; lift your voices in song,
> praising the Lord for all his works (39.12–14).

The theme to be developed with praise, with songs, with harps and with thanksgiving is:

All that the Lord has made is very good;
all that he commands will happen in due time (39.16).

Chapters 42.15–43.33 contain a lengthy hymn praising the
wonders of a universe which reflects the unfathomable glory of
God, a creation of order and contrast, sun and moon, stars and
rainbow, snow and hail, thunder and wind, scorching heat and
the deep with its 'strange and wonderful creatures', a hymn
which climaxes with the words:

Honour the Lord to the best of your ability,
and he will still be high above all praise.
Summon all your strength to declare his greatness,
and be untiring, for the most you can do will fall short.
Has anyone ever seen him, to be able to describe him?
Can anyone praise him as he truly is?
We have seen but a small part of his works,
and there remain many mysteries greater still.
The Lord has made everything
and has given wisdom to the godly (43.30–33).

In many respects this hymn contains echoes of the divine
speeches in Job 38ff.

An instruction section containing various maxims on contrasting attitudes to and different experiences of life leads Sirach into a
prayer addressed to the 'Lord, Father and Ruler of my life' (23.1;
cf. v.4), a prayer in which he asks for a proper ordering and
control of his own mind and senses. He may comment on the
weaknesses of others, but he is aware of his own weaknesses and
he brings them to God in prayer. After a discussion in 35.12–20 of
the justice and mercy of a God who exalts the humble and crushes
the merciless, particularly the pagan oppressors of God's people,
Sirach breaks into a prayer (36.1–17) which has close affinities
with the community laments in the Psalms, with its plea to God to
have pity upon his servants and to pour out his anger upon their
enemies. When we come to the epilogue to the book it begins in
51.1–12 with a Psalm of thanksgiving which is rich in echoes of
words and phrases from some of the thanksgiving Psalms. The
Hebrew text of Sirach inserts immediately after this passage a
fifteen line canticle, each line beginning with a call to praise, and
ending with the refrain from Psalm 136 'for his steadfast love lasts

for ever'. For a variety of reasons this section is unlikely to be authentic to Sirach,[4] but it is not out of character with his approach as a whole. Here is a wisdom teacher who never forgets that:

> Worship is out of place on the lips of a sinner,
> unprompted as he is by the Lord.
> Worship is the outward expression of wisdom,
> and the Lord himself inspires it (15.9–10).

3. But worship is not merely another element placed within a wisdom framework; we can also see how being steeped in the life of worship and prayer influenced Sirach's handling of specific issues. Let us take just two examples. (*a*) Like earlier wisdom writers Sirach issues warnings about the dangers and indeed the self-destructiveness of anger and quick temper. Thus:

> Unjust rage can never be excused;
> when anger tips the scale it is a man's downfall
>   (1.22; cf. Prov. 15.1; 27.4).

But his thoughts on anger and the desire for vengeance which rises from it in 27.30ff. take us far beyond this ethical stance to words which have their counterpart in the New Testament:

> Forgive your neighbour his wrongdoing;
> then, when you pray, your sins will be forgiven.
> If a man harbours a grudge against another,
> is he to expect healing from the Lord?
> If he has no mercy on his fellow-man,
> is he still to ask forgiveness for his own sins?
> If a mere mortal cherishes rage,
> where is he to look for pardon?
> Think of the end that awaits you, and have done with
>   hate;
> think of mortality and death, and be true to the
>   commandments;
> think of the commandments, and do not be enraged at
>   your neighbour;
> think of the covenant of the Most High, and overlook
>   faults (28.2–7).

(*b*) When he comes to discuss the relationship between sacrifice and daily life, Sirach is in the mainstream Old Testament tradition represented in the wisdom teaching and in the prophets (e.g. I Sam. 15.22; Amos 5.21–24; Hos. 6.6; Prov. 15.8; 21.3), in insisting that obedience to God is better than sacrifice: thus

> A sacrifice derived from ill-gotten gains is contaminated,
> a lawless mockery that cannot win approval (34.18).

But he is not content to leave it there. He is concerned with the positive significance of sacrifice. Yes, you must renounce evil, he says:

> Yet do not appear before the Lord empty-handed;
> perform these sacrifices because they are commanded.
> When the just man brings his offering of fat to the altar,
> its fragrance rises to the presence of the Most High.
> The just man's sacrifice is acceptable;
> it will never be forgotten.
> Be generous in your worship of the Lord
> and present the firstfruits of your labour in full measure.
> Give all your gifts cheerfully
> and be glad to dedicate your tithe.
> Give to the Most High as he has given to you,
> as generously as you can afford (35.4–10).

Sacrifice may be something commanded, but it is not to be offered in a spirit of carping obedience; gladness and generosity are key concepts in his approach to God. Thus in the pages of Sirach, teacher and worshipper walk hand in hand, and Sirach would have been a different kind of teacher if worship had not been central to his life.

Let us now try to examine the implications of this for certain of the issues in the relationship between wisdom and worship which we have been examining in earlier chapters.

1. What is wisdom and where is it to be found? Sirach begins with a passage which thematically takes us back to the poem on wisdom in Job 28. First, wisdom in its fullest sense, he claims, remains inaccessible to man's discovery or control:

Who can count the sand of the sea,
the drops of rain, or the days of unending time?
Who can measure the height of the sky,
the breadth of the earth, or the depth of the abyss?
Wisdom was first of all created things;
intelligent purpose has been there from the beginning.
Who has laid bare the root of wisdom?
Who has understood her subtlety? (1.2–6)

and secondly, it is God alone who knows the origin and the nature of wisdom:

One alone is wise, the Lord most terrible,
seated upon his throne.
It is he who created her, surveyed her and measured her,
and infused her into all his works (1.8–9).

From this God of wisdom wisdom comes as a gift in some measure to all mankind, 'but in plenty to those who love him' (1.10). This places wisdom firmly in a universalistic context – it is an interest and characteristic of all peoples. But it also makes a claim for a deeper and distinctive appreciation of wisdom within the context of Israel's life and faith. This theme of wisdom, open to some extent to all, but 'inherently private'[5] to Israel, is developed in wisdom's speech in chapter 24, where wisdom claims:

The waves of the sea, the whole earth,
every people and nation were under my sway.
Among them all I looked for a home:
in whose territory was I to settle? (24.6–7)

By God's decree the answer was Israel:

. . . Make your home in Jacob;
find your heritage in Israel (v.8)

and, in particular – and this fits in with Sirach's emphasis on worship – wisdom's presence is to be in Zion, in Jerusalem (vv.10–11), not because of any inherent goodness or perceptiveness in Israel, but simply because this was the people:

. . . whom the Lord had honoured
by choosing them to be his special possession (v.12).

But even among those who love her in Israel wisdom does not bestow her gifts easily or indiscriminately. Those who follow her she leads at first along tortuous paths:

> At first she will lead him by devious ways,
> filling him with craven fears.
> Her discipline will be a torment to him,
> and her decrees a hard test
> until he trusts her with all his heart.
> Then she will come straight back to him again and
> gladden him,
> and reveal her secrets to him.
> But if he strays from her, she will desert him
> and abandon him to his fate (4.17–19).

This could be read as a reflection of the advice which the friends shower on Job (e.g. 3.17–18): or as a comment on Job's own experience, led by devious ways through fear, torment and hard testing to an ultimate trust. Sirach returns to this theme in chapter 6 where, using an agricultural metaphor, he encourages the young to accept wisdom's discipline:

> Come to her like a farmer ploughing and sowing;
> then wait for her plentiful harvest.
> If you cultivate her, you will labour for a little while,
> but soon you will be eating her crops.
> How harsh she seems to the undisciplined (6.19–20a).

The person who seeks wisdom is then invited to:

> Put your feet in wisdom's fetters
> and your neck into her collar.
> Stoop to carry her on your shoulders
> and do not chafe at her bonds (6.24–25).

Submit to this burden and you will find the relief and the rest that wisdom has to offer:

> She will transform herself into joy for you.
> Her fetters will become your strong defence
> and her collar a gorgeous robe.
> Her yoke is a golden ornament

and her bonds a purple cord.
You shall put her on a like a gorgeous robe
and wear her like a splendid crown (6.28b–31; cf. Matt. 11.29).

Sirach gives similar advice to his intending pupils in 51.25:

> Bend your neck to the yoke,
> be ready to accept discipline;
> you need not go far to find it.

In all of this Sirach seems to be transposing the metaphysics of wisdom – its inaccessibility yet its presence as God's gift – into the experience of the person who seeks for wisdom, just as Israel's worship sought to hold in fruitful tension the sense of God's transcendence and yet his nearness to those who reached out to him (cf. Ps. 73). He is interested in exploring the inner dynamics of the search for wisdom, just as the psalmists explore the inner dynamics of faith in the context of worship.

2. We turn now to consider Sirach's use of the concept 'the fear of the Lord', particularly in its relationship to worship and to wisdom. As in earlier wisdom literature 'the fear of the Lord' is, for Sirach, the beginning (or the foundation) of wisdom (1.14; cf. Prov. 1.7; Job 28.28), and the link between 'the fear of the Lord' and wisdom is further developed in a series of pictures throughout chapter 1:

> Those who fear the Lord have their fill of wisdom;
> she gives them deep draughts of her wine (v.16).

> Wisdom's garland is the fear of the Lord,
> flowering with peace and health (v.18).

> Wisdom is rooted in the fear of the Lord,
> and long life grows on her branches (v.20).

> . . . the fear of the Lord is wisdom and discipline;
> fidelity and gentleness are his delight (v.27).

Indeed the fear of the Lord is claimed, by Sirach, to be the greatest of all gifts:

> How great is the man who finds wisdom!
> But no greater than he who fears the Lord.
> The fear of the Lord excels all other gifts;
> to what can we compare the man who has it? (25.10–11)

From it much of value in life flows. It is the guarantor of true friendship:

> A faithful friend is an elixir of life,
> found only by those who fear the Lord.
> The man who fears the Lord keeps his friendships in repair,
> for he treats his neighbour as himself (6.16–17).

It is the true basis of honour:

> What creature is worthy of honour? Man.
> What men? Those who fear the Lord.
> What creature is worthy of contempt? Man.
> What men? Those who break the commandments (10.19).

Honour may rightly be given to those who hold positions of authority in the community, 'but none of them is as great as the man who fears the Lord' (10.24). This passage also underlines what we have already seen to be true in Sirach's approach to wisdom, that there is for Sirach a close link between 'the fear of the Lord' and the commandments or torah in general (cf. 15.1; 32.14ff.). This is hardly novel (cf. Eccles. 12.13); nor is Sirach's emphasis, following earlier wisdom teaching and the Psalms, on the fear of the Lord and obedience, wisdom and the discipline of the wise, leading to success in worldly terms and their opposites leading to disaster. The fear of the Lord he says brings:

> . . . long life.
> Whoever fears the Lord will be prosperous at the last
> > (1.12b–13; cf. 11.22–23).

> Disaster never comes the way of the man who fears the Lord;
> in times of trial he will be rescued again and again (33.1),

which is no more and no less than Job's friends said (e.g. 5.19ff.). But what does Sirach mean by 'the fear of the Lord'? The fear of the Lord is an open-ended expression which can take on a variety of shades of meaning. Robert Gordis, for example, argued that when Koheleth invites his readers to 'fear God' (5.7) this is the statement of a man for whom faith in a living and gracious God has broken down, to be replaced by a primitive sense of dread.[6] In other contexts it seems to point to a vital sense of reverence or awe which finds expression in obedience to God. It is often argued that it is the nearest the Old Testament comes to having a word for religion or piety. But that merely leaves us asking, what kind of religion? There is little doubt as to the particular colouring which 'the fear of the Lord' has in Sirach. Long life may be associated with it in 1.12, but so also are 'exultation', 'cheerfulness and joy'. In chapter 7 it is linked with reverencing the priests and with loving your Maker with all your might (cf. 7.29–30). And it is closely associated with 'trusting in the Lord':

> Those who fear the Lord shall live,
> for their trust is in one who can keep them safe.
> The man who fears the Lord will have nothing else to fear;
> he will never be a coward, because his trust is in the Lord.
> How blest is the man who fears the Lord!
> He knows where to look for support.
> The Lord keeps watch over those who love him,
> their strong shield and firm support,
> a shelter from scorching wind and midday heat,
> a safeguard against stumbles and falls.
> He raises the spirits and makes the eyes sparkle,
> giving health, and life, and blessing (34.13–17).

As we saw in our earlier analysis of the *'ashre'* sayings[7] in the wisdom books and in the Psalms, this language of trusting in the Lord finds its natural setting not in wisdom sayings but in worship. When, therefore, in this passage Sirach says 'How blest is the man who fears the Lord' and links it with trusting in the Lord, this 'fear of the Lord' must be interpreted against the rich background of Sirach's life-time commitment to and his delight in worship. It is this which enables the fear of the Lord to be surrounded by words such as exultation, cheerfulness and joy. For Sirach there could be no teaching about the fear of the Lord which did not have its ultimate justification and its essential context in his experience of worship.

3. What of the problem of theodicy? There are passages in Sirach, which like certain material in earlier wisdom books seem to deny that there is a problem:

You who fear the Lord, wait for his mercy;
do not stray or you will fall.
You who fear the Lord, trust in him,
and you shall not miss your reward.
You who fear the Lord, expect prosperity,
lasting happiness and favour.
Consider the past generations and see:
was anyone who trusted the Lord ever disappointed?
was anyone who stood firm in the fear of him ever deserted?
did he ever neglect anyone who prayed to him?
For the Lord is compassionate and merciful;
he forgives sins and comes to the rescue in time of trouble
(2.7–10).[8]

None of Job's friends spoke with greater confidence, but it was not a confidence Job shared.

Of the other two ways in which earlier tradition in Israel sought to side-step the problem[9] neither was possible for Sirach. Amid the plurality of gods in the Hellenistic world there could be no compromising his monotheistic stance; and his strong commitment to worship and prayer, his sense of the presence of God, meant that he could hardly walk along the path taken by Koheleth. What is clear, however, is that Sirach is well aware that he is living in a world which has a lively interest in questions concerning the character and the purposes of God, and that many traditional religious assumptions were being challenged. J. Crenshaw[10] has drawn attention to the occurrence in Sirach of an ancient debate form found in Egyptian texts and once in Koheleth 7.10, a form which has three standard elements, (*a*) an introductory, 'Do not say', (*b*) a direct quotation of the unacceptable opinion, and (*c*) a refutation introduced by the word *ki*, that is 'for'. Thus in chapter 5 we find:

Do not say, 'I am my own master';
(for) you may be sure the Lord will call you to
account (5.3).

Do not say, 'I sinned, yet nothing happened to me';
(for) it is only that the Lord is very patient (5.4).

Do not say, 'His mercy is so great,
he will pardon my sins, however many.'

> (for) to him belong both mercy and wrath,
> and sinners feel the weight of his retribution (5.6).

The attitude here attacked is reminiscent of the attitude of the wicked in Psalm 73 and other Psalms, who arrogantly defy God and say:

> What does God know? The Most High neither knows nor
> cares (Ps. 73.11).

Sirach's response here underlines, against the background of God's patience, the certainty of retribution, and the fact that it may come, as he asserts in verse 7, suddenly and unexpectedly (cf. Ps. 73.18–20). A similar line of argument is to be found in 16.17:

> Do not say, 'I am hidden from the Lord;
> who is there in heaven to give a thought to me?
> Among so many I shall not be noticed;
> what is my life compared with the measureless creation?'

Here the argument seems to be the opposite from that found in Psalm 8: in the total context of the universe, people are arguing that man is so insignificant that he is not worth God's notice. The refutation in this case takes the form of an extended statement of God's control over the entire universe, heaven and earth, the very foundations of the world, which tremble when he looks upon them (v.19), a control often secretly at work:

> As a squall takes men unawares,
> so most of his (i.e. God's) works are done in
> secret (16.21).

To think otherwise, and to deny God's justice, says Sirach:

> . . . are the thoughts of a small mind,
> the absurdities of a senseless and misguided man (16.23).

This response is consistent with the great hymns in which he celebrates the unfathomable wisdom and glory of God (see above). To live without a sense of mystery is for Sirach the mark of a petty mind.

In 15.11–12 we find a different argument:

Do not say, 'The Lord is to blame for my failure';
(for) it is for you to avoid doing what he hates.
Do not say, 'It was he who led me astray';
(for) he has no use for sinful men.

Here the argument is against a form of determinism which attributed evil directly to God or to 'Fate' – a common idea in the Hellenistic world – and thus denied human responsibility. There are two objections to this in Sirach's mind. First, it involves a fatal misunderstanding of the nature of God:

The Lord hates every kind of vice;
you cannot love it and still fear him (15.13).

Such a God can never, then, be held responsible for evil. Secondly, it nullifies the repeated wisdom contrast between the wise and the foolish, the righteous and the wicked, a contrast which presupposes man's ability to choose, an ability which Sirach claims is God-given:

When he made man in the beginning,
he left him free to take his own decisions;
if you choose, you can keep the commandments;
whether or not you keep faith is yours to decide.
He has set before you fire and water;
reach out and take which you choose;
before man lie life and death,
and whichever he prefers is his (15.14–17).

Sirach can neither accept a cold, indifferent and disorderly universe nor a morally irresponsible God nor the denial of human freedom. At this point his denials are not rooted in philosophical argument, but in the presuppositions of the great didactic poems and hymns to which we have referred. For Sirach, therefore, the problem of theodicy is insoluble outside the context of worship with its call to praise the creator. It has been argued that Sirach has a further contribution to make to the problem of theodicy on a psychological level by claiming that 'the wicked are victims of great *Angst*, of nightmares and of constant worry and grief',[11] a judgment largely based on 40.1–11 with its thesis that mental disturbance is part of human experience and, in particular, the lot of the wicked. But this hardly seems to me to be relevant. The problem only becomes acute, as it does in Job, when such *Angst* and mental disturbance come not to the wicked but to the righteous, and can in no way be regarded as a punishment for sin.

4. Within the context of questions being raised about the meaning and significance of human life, Sirach's thoughts never stray very far from the reality of death. Within the carefully balanced complex of opposites built into the God-given structure of creation death stands as the opposite to life:

> All men alike come from the ground;
> Adam was created out of earth.
> Yet in his great wisdom the Lord distinguished them
> and made them go various ways:
> some he blessed and lifted high,
> some he hallowed and brought near to himself,
> some he cursed and humbled
> and removed from their place.
> As clay is in the potter's hands,
> to be moulded just as he chooses,
> so are men in the hands of their Maker,
> to be dealt with as he decides.
> Good is the opposite of evil, and life of death;
> yes, and the sinner is the opposite of the godly.
> Look at all the works of the Most High:
> they go in pairs, one the opposite of the other (33. 10–17).

Men may be different, successful or failures, good or evil, sinners or godly, but all experience the fear of death (40.5) and all stand under the one sentence: '. . . You shall die' (14.17). Since no one knows when death will strike, *now* is the time for maximizing your activities and enjoying what you have:

> Remember that death is not to be postponed;
> the hour of your appointment with the grave is undisclosed.
> Before you die, do good to your friend;
> reach out as far as you can to help him.
> Do not miss a day's enjoyment
> or forgo your share of innocent pleasure.
> Are you to leave to others all you have laboured for
> and let them draw lots for your hard-earned wealth?
>
> (14.12–15; cf. 11.18–19)

There are strong echoes here of the teaching of Koheleth.[12]

And beyond death? Nothing. Sirach is shrewd enough to argue that this nothingness is preferable to some of the bitter experiences of life:

> Better death than a life of misery,
> eternal rest than a long illness (30.17).

Death indeed is preferable to being an incorrigible fool:

> Mourn over the dead for the eclipse of his light;
> mourn over the fool for the eclipse of his wits.
> Mourn less bitterly for the dead, for he is at rest;
> but the fool's life is worse than death.
> Mourning for the dead lasts seven days,
> but for a godless fool it lasts all his life (22.11–12; cf. 28.22).

The fact of death, however, is used by Sirach in two very positive ways.

(a) Death should determine the quality of life *now*. Sirach uses it to back up a plea for responsible living. His plea for generosity and kindness, for sharing in the grief of others and visiting the sick, is capped by the words:

> Whatever you are doing, remember the end that awaits you;
> then all your life you will never go wrong (7.36).

Arrogance and injustice are unacceptable in individual or national conduct:

> What has man to be so proud of? He is only dust and ashes,
> subject even in life to bodily decay.
> A long illness mocks the doctor's skill;
> today's king is tomorrow's corpse.
> When a man dies, he comes into an inheritance
> of maggots and vermin and worms (10.9–11).

The thought of death likewise gives added force to the call to repent:

> Turn back to the Lord and have done with sin;
> make your prayer in his presence, and so lessen your offence.
> Come back to the Most High, renouncing wrongdoing,
> and hate intensely what he abhors.

Who will praise the Most High in the grave
in place of the living who give him thanks?
When a man is dead and ceases to be, his gratitude dies
    with him;
it is when he is alive and well that he praises the Lord
                                 (17.25–28).

(*b*) The inevitable frailty and transitoriness of human life
functions in Sirach, as it does in some of the Psalms (e.g. Ps. 103.
13–18), as the basis for a theology firmly grounded in the
patience, the love and the forgiveness of God. We have already
had occasion to note the different ways in which the question
'What is man?' is handled in Psalms 8 and 144 and in Job 7. Sirach
raises the same question in 18.8:

What is man and what use is he?
What do his good or evil deeds signify?

As in Psalm 144 the question is answered in words which
underline man's transitoriness and insignificance:

His span of life is at the most a hundred years;
compared with endless time, his few years
are like one drop of sea-water or a single grain of sand
                                 (18.9–10).

Far from this leading God to ignore man, however, or to dismiss
him as unimportant, Sirach argues:

This is why the Lord is patient with them,
lavishing his mercy upon them.
He sees and knows the harsh fate in store for
them,
and therefore gives full play to his forgiveness.
Man's compassion is only for his neighbour,
but the Lord's compassion is for every living thing
                              (18.11–13).

While others, by the time Sirach was writing, particularly in
apocalyptic circles, were developing a doctrine of resurrection to
counter and redress the harsh fate that had befallen God's people
in the world, Sirach uses the 'harsh fate' of death to underline the
nature of God's forgiveness and compassion in the here and now.

There is no evidence that Sirach parts company from the traditional picture of Sheol as we have seen it in both the wisdom literature and in the Psalms; but he shows how, far from being merely chill and negative, it can be used constructively both in ethics and in theology.

So many of the strands which we have previously analysed in the wisdom and worship traditions of ancient Israel seem to come together, closely interwoven in the fabric of the thinking of Sirach, who is both teacher and worshipper. What is missing in Sirach is the urgent search for meaning as it expresses itself in the repeated 'whys?' that we find in the Psalms, in Job and Koheleth. He may reflect on the *Angst* of the wicked, but he himself seems to have been singularly free from *Angst*. He could not be like Koheleth, since the praise of God and the pull of worship were central to his life. He could not be like Job since life seems to have dealt kindly with him. To those who have never been stretched to breaking point he still has much to say; to those who have been so stretched, his wisdom and his approach to worship need to be supplemented by the cries of more perplexed worshippers.

Chapter 8

Songs of God's People –
Then and Now

This last chapter is in the form of an epilogue. Like the epilogue to the book of Job, its purpose is to try to draw together and assess the significance of some of the threads in the material we have been examining. Scholars, of course, have expressed the most diverse reactions to the epilogue to the book of Job. Some regard it as thoroughly unsatisfactory, an attempt to crawl back into comforting certainties which much of the rest of the book has been trying to destroy. You may well feel likewise at the end of this chapter. So be it.

We have been attempting to analyse the relationship between the wisdom literature and the worship tradition in ancient Israel up to and including Jesus ben Sirach at the beginning of the second century BCE. Although theological issues have been central to the discussion, we have been involved in what could be regarded as a purely historical exercise. If indeed we had been dealing with material solely from ancient Egypt or Babylonia we might have been content to leave it there, while recognizing that there are lessons to be drawn from all historical study. The relevant material, however, from ancient Israel comes down to us as part of a still living tradition of faith. Whether in its Jewish or its Christian form, it comes as scripture, as part of a Canon.[1] This forces us to look at the material in another light, since as James A. Sanders puts it, 'It is the nature of the Canon to be contemporized: it is not primarily a source book for the history of Israel, early Judaism, Christ or the Christian Church, but rather a mirror for the identity of the believing community which, in every era, turns to it to ask who it is and what it is to do, even today.'[2] We must therefore try to ask, however inadequately, what has this study of wisdom and worship in the Old Testament to do with us today, with our understanding of ourselves and our world, and with what we ought to be doing within a community of faith which claims to have its roots in the biblical material. The move from ancient texts to where we are today is not so easy as we sometimes pretend, and any simplistic use of the Bible which ignores its historical and cultural conditioning can do more harm than good.[3] We must, therefore, begin by acknowledging that there are significant differences, cultural and sociological, between the world which nurtured the wisdom literature of the Old Testament and our world today. In particular, there is one fundamental difference between the intellectual tradition represented by Old Testament wisdom and the intellectual tradition in which we stand today. We have argued that there never was in ancient Israel a purely secular wisdom tradition. Wisdom always operated within the context of certain religious constraints. This is self-evidently not true today. Atheism and agnosticism are part and parcel of today's intellectual world in a way in which they were not, and could not have been, in ancient Israel even among its most radically sceptical thinkers – for example Koheleth. David Daiches in *God and the Poets* has interestingly traced the impact of this development in poetry, and the profound effect it had upon poetry in the nineteenth century when poets no longer had any sure point of reference outside themselves and their world, even when such poetry could be described as religious.[4] Recognizing that this is so, and that 'the fear of the Lord' is, by and large, an unknown factor or at best an optional ingredient in the modern pursuit of wisdom, what can we say about Israel's contribution? The legitimate interface between philosophy and religion or science and religion are not areas into which I have any competence to enter: instead I want to look at what we might and perhaps ought to be doing in this context within the life of the church and particularly in our approach to worship.

1. The wisdom writers in Israel had a lively interest in the world around them. This is the raw material from which they draw their illustrations and upon which they pass their comments. Sirach, for example, may wish above all else to commend:

> The man who devotes himself
> to studying the law of the Most High,
> who investigates all the wisdom of the past (39.1),

but he has a keen interest in other activities; in the skill of doctors, 'finding a cure to save their patient's life' (38.14), in craftsmen and designers, 'who make engravings on signets, and patiently vary the design' (38.27), in the smith, 'sitting by his anvil, intent on his iron-work' (38.28), in the potter, 'turning the wheel with his feet' (38.29). All these, he says

> . . . maintain the fabric of this world,
> and their daily work is their prayer (38.34).[5]

Had he been living in our world Sirach would no doubt have expanded his list to include people like computer operators, nuclear physicists, bioengineers, biochemists, astrophysicists, novelists, playwrights, radio and TV producers, etc. Alongside of this, recall how the issues with which the wise wrestled in Israel *in their day*, found expression in the Psalms and were thus taken into the context of worship, and ask to what extent is there evidence of this happening today? Am I wrong in thinking that on the whole the answer to that question must be 'depressingly little'? Certainly my experience of worship is that on the average Sunday the congregation may be singing hymns drawn from many centuries of Christian devotion, but the cut-off point is usually the nineteenth century, and even when we sing twentieth-century hymns very few of them seem to take any cognizance of the intellectual and social revolution through which we have been living. Analyse the prayers, and give or take some modification of language – 'you's rapidly replacing 'thou's and 'thee's – most of the prayers would have been equally acceptable and appropriate a hundred years ago. In other words, the wisdom of today, the intellectual ferment in which we are all involved, flows strongly all around us, yet our forms of worship remain largely untouched. Now I have no desire to be iconoclastic, nor to question the continuing value of the rich heritage of hymns and prayers which sustain the life of the church, whether they come from Augustine, Thomas à Kempis, Luther, Cranmer, the Scottish metrical Psalms or the Wesleys. My only plea is for something else more closely related to and reflecting the world in which God has chosen to place us today. And it can be done. The title of this chapter was partly influenced by the publication in 1988 of a supplement to the Church of Scotland Church Hymnary (third edition) entitled *Songs of God's People*.[6] In some ways it is a curious mixture – the resurrection of old favourites omitted in the last edition of the Hymnary, evangelistic choruses, folk material from the world church, particularly Africa; but there are also hymns which seriously seek to bring to worship the world in which we are living today. Let me give you two examples. The first, set to a traditional Scottish melody, Dream Angus, is by John Bell and Graham Maule of the Iona Community Worship Group.

After an opening verse which affirms that 'Christ's is the world in which we move' and a chorus which ends with the line 'Christ makes with his friends a touching place' verses two to four are as follows:

> 2. Feel for the people we most avoid –
>   strange or bereaved or never employed.
>   Feel for the women and feel for the men
>   who fear that their living is all in vain.

> 3. Feel for the parents who've lost their child,
>   feel for the women whom men have defiled,
>   feel for the baby for whom there's no breast
>   and feel for the weary who find no rest.

> 4. Feel for the lives by life confused,
>   riddled with doubt, in loving abused;
>   feel for the lonely heart, conscious of sin,
>   which longs to be pure but fears to begin.[7]

That hymn puts into the context of worship the confused human relationships, the pressures in society today.

Here is another hymn which focusses more on the ecological issues confronting creation today:

> 1. Lord bring the day to pass,
>   when forest, rock and hill,
>   the beasts, the birds, the grass,
>   will know thy finished will;
>   when man attains his destiny
>   and nature its lost unity.

2. Forgive our careless use
   of water, ore and soil –
   the plenty we abuse
   supplied by others' toil;
   save us from making self our creed,
   turn us toward each other's need.

3. Give us, when we release
   creation's secret powers,
   to harness them for peace,
   our children's peace and ours:
   teach us the art of mastering
   which makes life rich and draws death's sting.

4. Creation groans, travails,
   futile its present plight,
   bound – till the hour it hails
   God's children born of light
   who enter on their true estate.
   Come, Lord: new heavens and earth create.[8]

This is bringing to God in worship two of the issues which *must* impinge upon our thinking today – our handling of the environment and the nuclear threat to life.

When we turn to prayers, one of the most helpful collections I have come across is *Be our Freedom Lord* edited by Terry Falla,[9] responsive prayers for contemporary worship. Here is part of a prayer on the same theme as the last hymn:

Great God our Father, we believe that
our worship draws us to you
and towards our neighbours on earth.

We pray for the whole creation:

May we learn before it is too late
to respect the uniqueness, fragility and beauty
of our earth and all its creatures.

We pray for every nation and race:

May our actions and lifestyle bear out our belief
that all people everywhere are our brothers and sisters,
whatever their country, their city, or their tribe,
whatever their education or their culture,

whatever their circumstances, religion or colour.
We pray for peace in our torn and troubled world:

We pray that weapons may be discarded instead of people,
guns silenced instead of the voices of the poor,
and that in a world half-expecting nuclear holocaust,
we might learn that love is not a luxury.[10]

This is not a plea that we should take the mystery and mystique
out of worship by merely fitting it into the world or limiting our
horizons to contemporary problems. Just as the wisdom tradition
in the Old Testament was well aware that at the heart of wisdom
there was a mystery accessible only to God, so worship in Israel
again and again sought to communicate that sense of mystery. Is
it not precisely here that there may be a point of contact between
worship and the search for wisdom in our world today? Whether
they are religious or not there are few philosophers or scientists
today who wish to dispense with the concept of mystery. Many
scientists would be the first to admit that what they are doing is
'to build little islands of rationality in a universe which is deeply
mysterious'[11] – and some would say becoming ever more
mysterious. There is, of course, a difference at this point between
the recognition of mystery in modern thought and in the biblical
tradition. Commenting on Psalm 139 G. von Rad said: 'The
whole Psalm indeed is a paradigm of the intermingling of faith
and knowledge. The desire for knowledge is so pressing that, at
the limits which are imposed upon it, it becomes witness to God's
inscrutability . . . But one must never lose sight of the fact that
the wise men never speak in a narrow sense of the mystery of the
world. The mysteries of the world have no independent existence. In them man directly confronts the mystery of God. Israel's
intellectual powers have never escaped from the shadow of the
great mystery of God.'[12]

Modern man's intellectual powers have escaped from the
shadow of the great mystery of God, but still are left facing
mystery which often they do not know how to handle. Martin
Dalby, Head of Music for BBC Scotland, once drew a parallel
between music and religion. Both he claimed try to touch the
senses with the magic of wonder; then he added 'Bad religion
answers the unanswerable; great religion cherishes the mystery.'
For religion in that statement substitute worship and we are

saying something important about the relevance of worship in our world today. In this context the banality of certain styles of worship today is depressing, particularly when they are offered to us on the plea of relevance to the world, as if once worship had become demythologized it would somehow be rationally acceptable. Wisdom and worship in Israel today join hands when they have room for the issues which life presents to them, but at the same time 'cherish the mystery' which lies at the heart of all life.

2. We have noted the extent to which there is built into both the wisdom literature and the Psalms what we have called 'the search for meaning',[13] centring upon the raising of questions, the agonized 'whys?' and 'how longs?' of the Psalms and Job. These are questions which are concerned not merely with the ultimate mystery of God, of how he acts or fails to act, whether he is just or unjust, but also questions about the meaning, the worthwhileness of human life. The centrality of such questioning not only in the limited field we have been exploring, but more widely across the Old Testament – as I tried to demonstrate in *The Courage to Doubt* – makes me deeply suspicious of an approach to faith and worship which seems to deal only with answers and certainties, and not with questions and perplexities. Matthew Arnold's poem, 'Dover Beach', written in 1867, has been regarded by many as giving classic expression to the relentless retreat from religious certainties and dogma in the face of advancing knowledge:

> The Sea of Faith
> Was once, too, at the full, and round earth's shore
> Lay like the folds of a bright girdle furled;
> But now I only hear
> Its melancholy, long, withdrawing roar
> Retreating, to the breath
> Of the night-wind, down the vast edges drear
> And naked shingle of the world.

John Habgood comments: 'Matthew Arnold got it wrong. God is not away there in the retreating sea, an ever more distant vision leaving us stranded on the shingle. God is in the turbulence which rages inside us. God is in the questioning, in the agonizing.'[14] But if God is in the questioning, in the agonizing, there is not much evidence of this in our approach to worship. I listen to prayers inviting God to 'forgive us our doubts' and wonder how many people's guilt complexes in the congregation are being compounded. I seldom hear prayers asking forgiveness for our failure to question our superficial and blinkered certainties. I join in hymns which point me to:

> A faith that shines more bright and clear
> When tempests rage without,
> That when in danger knows no fear,
> In darkness feels no doubt,

a hymn whose last line has alway seemed to me a typical nineteenth-century sentimentalizing of an emphasis which is correctly voiced in Luther's great hymn 'A safe stronghold our God is still'. Or I am invited to join in singing a hymn whose last verse assures us:

> If our love were but more simple
> we should take him at his word,
> and our lives would be all sunshine
> in the sweetness of our Lord.

If such hymns are the last or the only word, then the book of Job should never have been written, and it is hard to see how questioning and agonizing can be anything other than lack of faith. To say this may be consistent with other scriptures, perhaps with the Koran, but hardly with the Bible as containing the word of God for us. There should be room in hymns and prayers for people to identify themselves with a tradition of faith which affirms that God is with them, in the questioning and in the doubts with which they are struggling. Let me again illustrate what I mean. Hymn 116 in *Songs of God's People* explores this struggling:

> 1. When our confidence is shaken
>   in beliefs we thought secure;
>   when the spirit in its sickness
>   seeks but cannot find a cure:
>   God is active in the tensions
>   of a faith not yet mature.

2. Solar systems, void of meaning,
   freeze the spirit into stone;
   always our researches lead us
   to the ultimate unknown:
   faith must die, or come full circle
   to its source in God alone.

3. In the discipline of praying,
   when it's hardest to believe;
   in the drudgery of caring,
   when it's not enough to grieve:
   faith, maturing, learns acceptance
   of the insights we receive.

4. God is love; and he redeems us
   in the Christ we crucify:
   this is God's eternal answer
   to the world's eternal why;
   may we in this faith maturing
   be content to live and die![15]

Here is a part of a prayer from *Be our Freedom Lord*, a prayer entitled 'He is Hidden':

Why God? Why? Why, when our need
is desperate, when all other help is vain,
do you turn away from us?

Why? Why, when the darkness is deepest
and our midnight is starless,
do you hide yourself from us?

Why, in times of grief and distress,
when there is no light in the window,
do we find a door slammed in our face,
and a sound of bolting and
double bolting on the inside?

Why forsake us when we need you most?
Why are you present when the skies are clear,
our help in days of prosperity,
but so absent in our time of trouble?

Why, like your servant Job, do you give us
reason to feel that 'Were he to pass me,
I should not see him', like your prophet
Jeremiah to feel deceived, angry, desolate?

We know that faith does not exempt us from sorrow
or shield us from evil – we know that; we know too,
that the earth is wet with the blood of the innocent –
but why this? Why now? Why?

Know this, God, know this: if faith were dependent
on feelings, if our trust in you were no more than
a matter of the mind, we would have done with you,
done with you now, done with you for ever.

The prayer ends:

God of Christ,
God who raised him from the dead,
God with whom life can begin again,
come to us now, hold us, help us, heal us,
for you and you alone are our salvation.

That prayer expresses confidence that there is healing to be
found in the midst of questioning, but it is healing asked for by
those who know their need for healing since they are seeking
honestly to wrestle with issues to which there are no easy
answers. That is why in the end Job is healed and his friends are
on the receiving end of God's anger: that is why the urgent cries
for God to respond, and the probing of problems and doubts
which call his care and his power into question have such a
prominent place among the Psalms. There is no 'wisdom' today
which can take refuge in blind optimism – the ecological crisis,
the nuclear threat to life, the clamant cries for justice within
society and among the nations make such optimism impossible.
Nor should worship encourage us to a blind escapism from such
urgent issues. How can it when at the centre of Christian worship
is the mystery of the One who came to share our life and took
upon himself its pain, its suffering and its unanswered
questions? 'My God, my God, why have you forsaken me?' are
not the words of one for whom faith was simple and life all
sunshine. There will always be those who, in an age of increasing

perplexity, seek refuge in voices in church or in society who demand a total commitment which refuses to leave any space for questioning or doubt. But there ought to be a place within the church for those who bring their questions with them into commitment and seek within the community of faith to pursue their search for meaning, and equally a place for those who are not sure that they know what commitment means. For such people, worship, I believe, could be made more helpful than it often is.

3. We found in the wisdom writings and in the Psalms that there was no one answer to the questions which life posed. We heard in the wisdom books the voices of those who held on to the well-established belief that obedience to God brought tangible rewards in this world, and the voices of those who argued that life just did not follow this script. There were those who claimed that the wicked experienced and deserved swift punishment and an early death, while others insisted that there was no empirical evidence to support this belief. There were those untroubled by the problem of theodicy, and those who tried to unscramble it in a variety of different ways. And all these different views were there in the Psalms, finding expression in the context of worship. Furthermore we have argued that the wisdom approach to reality provided Israel not with a type of secular humanism, but with an alternative way of doing theology, a different way of speaking about God alongside theologies which concentrated on theophanies, on God speaking directly to man, or which focussed on the mighty acts of God in Israel's history. Again it is noteworthy that these different ways of speaking about God lie side by side within the Psalms. Thus Psalm 49 which, on any analysis, has strong links with the wisdom tradition, immediately follows Psalm 48, one of the Songs of Zion, which celebrates Jerusalem as 'the city of the Lord of hosts, a city which can never be destroyed by its and God's enemies'. Psalm 73, wrestling with the problem of theodicy and struggling to come to terms with what faith means, is immediately followed by Psalm 74, a community lament, which celebrates the mighty acts of God in the past, in creation and in history, as the grounds for an urgent appeal to God to intervene in the present. A hymn book which begins confidently affirming that:

> The Lord watches over the way of the righteous,
> but the way of the wicked is doomed (Ps. 1.6),

soon introduces us to a lament:

> How long, O Lord, will you forget me?
> How long will you hide your face from me?
> How long must I suffer anguish in my soul, grief in
> my heart, day and night?
> How long shall the enemy lord it over me? (Ps. 13.1–2)

– the words of a man who trusted in God, and who would naturally and rightly think of himself as belonging to the righteous rather than to the wicked. Such a rich catholicity of material, shared by the wisdom writers and the psalmists, and their acceptance of a pluralistic approach to theology have much to teach us. In the Christian community today we are faced with a multiplicity of theological perspectives, and even those who most vehemently deplore this – usually in the interests of insisting that their own perspective is the only legitimate perspective – can hardly deny that such multiplicity exists. Such perspectives range all the way from fundamentalist perspectives which seem to assume that there is only one biblical theology which only needs to be proclaimed with conviction to be effective, through traditionalists either Protestant or Roman Catholic who assume that the Reformation formulation of doctrine or the *Summa Theologiae* of Thomas Aquinas hold the key to the theological needs of today, all the way to the most radical of radicals who believe that all biblical ways of speaking about God are outmoded, and need to be demythologized and reinterpreted in terms of our human values. The trouble with such theological pluralism is that it tends to become increasingly divisive, with groups within the church absolutizing their own limited vision, 'by labelling perspectives different from their own as heretical or at least non-edifying. Such attempts fail to take seriously the common material within which we all belong, which accepts diversity and conflict, but also demands that we seek to learn from and integrate different perspectives and traditions into our own. To a certain extent, the biblical message, viewed as a whole, affirms that these other traditions are ours also.'[16] My only quarrel with that statement is to question the need for the words 'to a certain extent'. We must be prepared to affirm without equivocation that there are 'other traditions' within the biblical material to which we need to listen, particularly when they do not sit easily alongside the creative influences, or the prejudices, which have moulded our thinking.

This is not a plea for the blurring of differences, nor for avoiding a rigorous pursuit of truth. There is no blurring of the differences in the dialogue between Job and his friends. There is, on the part of Job, an agonizing search for a God who could only be found beyond or behind the theological certainties of the friends. We have already noted[17] the studied irony in Job 42.7 where God expresses his anger at the friends who 'have not spoken as you ought about me, as my servant Job has done', yet it is equally important to note that Job and his friends still remain within the one community of faith. The friends who had earlier repeatedly urged Job to throw himself upon the mercy of God, now find that they stand in need of that mercy: while Job, who had been bitterly critical of and increasingly alienated from his friends, now finds himself interceding on their behalf. And, as we have seen, the views of both Job and his friends are to be found side by side in Israel's tradition of worship as that has come down to us in the Psalms.

Worship ought to be the place where, in the midst of our different theological stances, be they traditional, radical or sceptical, we find our oneness in a common acceptance by God and a common reaching out for God. But that can only happen when we share the stance of Jesus ben Sirach and confess:

> However much we say, we cannot exhaust our theme;
> to put it into a word: he is all.
> Where can we find the skill to sing his praises?
> For he is greater than all his works.
> The Lord is terrible and very great,
> and marvellous is his power.
> Honour the Lord to the best of your ability,
> and he will still be high above all praise.
> Summon all your strength to declare his greatness,
> and be untiring, for the most you can do will fall short.
> Has anyone ever seen him, to be able to describe him?
> Can anyone praise him as he truly is? (Sirach 43.27–31)

This is to accept *our* limitations, that *our* life and *our* search for wisdom are bounded by mystery, a mystery which is not destroyed but deepened when it comes to us in one who, in Paul's words, is 'the power of God and the wisdom of God' (I Cor. 1.24). It is to make a plea for what John Habgood has called a 'necessary agnosticism', 'a proper recognition of the ultimate mysteriousness of God and the universe and the limitations of knowledge and the relativity of our standpoint',[18] not least in theology. And that is but a contemporary version of the question with which we began in Job 28.12:

> But where can wisdom be found?
> And where is the source of understanding?

with the necessary agnosticism in the poet's reply:

> No man knows the way to it,
> it is not found in the land of the living (Job 28.13).

Abbreviations

ANET   J. P. Pritchard (ed.), *Ancient Near Eastern Texts*
         Relating to the Old Testament, Princeton 1969
BZAW   Beihefte zur Zeitschrift für die alttestamentliche
         Wissenschaft, Berlin
GNB   Good News Bible
JBL   *Journal of Biblical Literature*, Philadelphia
KJB   King James Bible
NEB   New English Bible
NIV   New International Version
RSV   Revised Standard Version
SBT   Studies in Biblical Theology
SVT   Supplements to *Vetus Testamentum*, Leiden
VT   *Vetus Testamentum*, Leiden
ZAW   *Zeitschrift für die alttestamentliche Wissenschaft*, Berlin

Notes

1. What is Wisdom?

1. J. Blenkinsopp, *Wisdom and Law in the Old Testament*, Oxford 1983, p.134.
2. N. Habel, *The Book of Job* (Old Testament Library Series), London and Philadelphia 1985, p.391.
3. Ibid., introduction.
4. Blenkinsopp, op. cit., p.25.
5. D. F. Morgan, *Wisdom in the Old Testament Traditions*, Atlanta 1981, p.16: cf. J. L. Crenshaw (ed.), *Studies in Ancient Israelite Wisdom*, New York 1976.
6. J. Bright, *The Authority of the Old Testament*, London 1967, p.136.
7. E.g. W. G. Lambert, *Babylonian Wisdom Literature*, Oxford 1960. W. McKane, *Proverbs* (Old Testament Library Series) London and Philadelphia 1970.
8. R. N. Whybray, *The Intellectual Tradition in the Old Testament*, BZAW 135, Berlin 1974.
9. S. Talmon, 'Wisdom in the Book of Esther', *VT* XIII, 1963, pp.419–455.
10. M. Weinfeldt, *Deuteronomy and the Deuteronomic School*, Oxford 1977.
11. G. von Rad, *Old Testament Theology*, Edinburgh 1965.
12. J. L. Crenshaw, *A Whirlpool of Torment: Israelite Tradition of God as Oppressive Presence*, Philadelphia 1984: (ed.), *Theodicy in the Old Testament*, Philadelphia and London 1983.
13. Cf. Lambert, op. cit.
14. Ibid., pp.92ff.
15. L. G. Perdue, *Wisdom and Cult*, Missoula 1977.
16. Ibid., p.345.

2. Defining the Wisdom Element in the Psalms

1. Cf. L. G. Perdue, *Wisdom and Cult*, Missoula 1977.
2. S. Mowinckel, 'Psalms and Wisdom' in *Wisdom in Israel and in the Ancient Near East*, SVT 3, 1955, pp.205–224.
3. H. L. Janzen, *Die spätjudische Psalmdichtung*, Oslo 1937.
4. J. H. Kuntz, 'The Canonical Wisdom Psalms of Ancient Israel' in *Rhetorical Criticism: Essays in Honor of James Muilenburg*, Pittsburgh Theological Monograph Series, I, 1974, pp. 186–223.
5. R. E. Murphy, 'Wisdom – Theses and Hypotheses' in *Israelite Wisdom*.

Theological and Literary Essays in Honor of Samuel Terrien, ed. J. G. Gammie et. al., Missoula 1978.

6. *Wisdom and Cult*, Missoula, 1977.

7. Ibid., p.362.

8. Ibid., p.211.

9. Ibid., p.279.

10. Ibid., p.362.

11. *Scottish Metrical Paraphrases*, 1781.

12. D. F. Morgan. op. cit., pp.130–1.

13. J. Ross, 'Psalm 73' in *Israelite Wisdom*, p.170.

14. J. H. Kuntz, 'The Retributive Motif in Psalmic Wisdom' in *ZAW* 89, 1977, pp.223ff.

15. Deut. 33.29; I Kings 10.8; Isa. 30.18;32. 18;56.2; Dan. 12.2.

16. Contrast the NEB translation following G. R. Driver:

> When there is no one in authority, the people break loose,
> but a guardian of the law keeps them on the straight path.

See W. McKane, *Proverbs* ad loc. for a criticism of this rendering.

17. Cf. W. McKane, ibid., ad loc.

18. Ibid., ad loc.

19. There is very extensive use in the Psalms of the phrase 'trusting in the Lord', Hebrew *batah*, followed by the preposition *b*, e.g. Pss. 9.11; 13.6; 21.8; 22.5,6; 25.2; 26.1 etc.

3. Some Wisdom Psalms

1. *ANET*, pp.395–6.

2. E.g. A. A. Anderson, *Psalms 1* (New Century Bible) London 1972; A. R. Johnson, *The Vitality of the Individual in the Thought of Ancient Israel*, Cardiff 1964.

3. E.g. the collection of instruction verbs in verse 8 – *skl,ydh,y'as* – the imagery of the way (cf. Ps. 1.1; Prov. 1.19; 3.23 etc.). The invitation to learn is characteristic of Proverbs 1–9; cf. R. N. Whybray, *The Concept of Wisdom in Proverbs 1–9*, SBT 45, London 1965.

4. For the link between the 'righteous' and the 'upright' see the discussion on Psalm 33, pp.35f.

5. E. Gerstenberger, *Psalms, Part I, with an Introduction to Cultic Poetry*, Grand Rapids 1988, p.142.

6. Cf. S. J. L. Croft, *The Identity of the Individual in the Psalms*, Sheffield 1987, p.201, note 11, and his interesting if brief discussion of the wisdom psalms pp. 159–169. Croft identifies eleven psalms in which the 'I' is a wisdom teacher, but dates all of them to the post-exilic period, with the most unorthodox protest occurring in Psalm 39.

7. J. L. Crenshaw includes it in his list of wisdom psalms in *Studies in Ancient Israelite Wisdom*, New York 1975.

8. The only other references to God's storehouses in the Old Testament are to be found in the hymnic passage in Jeremiah 10.13 and in Psalm 135.7, cf. Sirach 43.14:

> Therefore the storehouses are opened
> and the clouds fly forth like birds.

9. Note the different approaches in the commentaries on the Psalms by A. A. Anderson (1972), M. Dahood (1965) and H. J. Kraus (1961). We follow in the main the analysis of E. Gerstenberger, op. cit., 1988.

10. The only other passage in the Old Testament in which the verb translated 'stand in awe of' (Hebrew *gur*) with reference to God occurs is Psalm 22.24, again in parallelism with 'fearing the Lord'.

11. Cf. W. McKane, *Prophets and Wise Men*, SBT 44, London 1965, for the contrast and clash between the prophetic 'word' and the counsel of the wise.

12. Outside the wisdom and cultic traditions the phrase occurs in Deut. 11.12 'the eyes of the Lord are always upon the land'. A powerful case, however, can be made for wisdom influence on Deuteronomy, e.g. M. Weinfeldt, *Deuteronomy and the Deuteronomic School*, Oxford 1972.

13. Gerstenberger, op. cit., p.145.

14. W. G. Lambert, *Babylonian Wisdom Literature*, p.66.

15. Even if we retain the Masoretic pointing 'they looked to him' in verse 5 (Hebrew 6), it is still a generalization based on the Psalmist's experience.

16. McKane, *Proverbs*, p.151.

17. Lambert, op. cit., pp.63ff.

18. *Per contra* the commentaries on the Psalms by Anderson, Dahood and Gerstenberger.

4. The Search for Meaning

1. Quoted by J. L. Crenshaw, *Old Testament Wisdom: an Introduction*, Atlanta and London 1982, p.19.

2. This is the major theme of my earlier study *The Courage to Doubt*, London 1983, Philadelphia 1989.

3. *ANET*, pp.407f.

4. Ibid., line 68.

5. Ibid., p.467 cf. Ecclesiastes 3.19–22; 5.18.

6. Ibid., p.589.

7. Ibid., p.509, lines 42–45.

8. Ibid., lines 96–100.

9. W. G. Lambert, *Babylonian Wisdom Literature* p.27. A more recent study by Lambert in *AOS* 67, 1987, pp.187–201 notes that the sufferer acknowledges that he must have sinned. He concludes that the material is 'similar to complaint psalms which have never been classified as "wisdom"', p.201.

10. Lambert, *Babylonian Wisdom Literature*, loc. cit., Tablet II line 24.

11. Ibid., lines 33–38.

12. Ibid., p.75, line 58.

13. Ibid., p.89, lines 276–280.

14. Ibid., p.89, lines 295–297.

15. Expression is given to questions in the Psalms more than a hundred times.

16. E.g. N. Habel, *The Book of Job*, p.164.

17. D. Daiches, *God and the Poets*, Oxford 1984, p.48.

18. For detail see the commentaries by Anderson, Dahood and Gerstenberger.

19. This, the NEB translation, involves a slight alteration to the Hebrew text which at the beginning of the line reads an imperative 'Wait for God'. It does not, however, materially alter the meaning.

5. The Problem of Theodicy

1. C. W. J. Leibnitz, *Essais de theodicee*, Amsterdam 1910.
2. See the *Shorter Oxford English Dictionary*.
3. J. L. Crenshaw (ed.), *Theodicy in the Old Testament*, Philadelphia and London 1983, p.1.
4. Eichrodt, in *Theodicy in the Old Testament*, p.17.
5. D. Daiches, *God and the Poets*, Oxford 1984, p.3.
6. Ibid., p.25.
7. *Theodicy in the Old Testament*, p.36.
8. See *The Courage to Doubt*.
9. See texts quoted in Chapter 4 above.
10. *ANET*, p.418.
11. Ibid., p.420.
12. Ibid., p.369.
13. For an excellent discussion of this issue see Daiches, op. cit., chapter two 'God Defended', pp.26–49.
14. Cf. 'The Dispute of a Man with his Ba' and 'The Song of the Harper' in both of which the uncertainty as to what happens at death reinforces the appeal to enjoy life while it lasts.
15. See pp.49–50.
16. *ANET* p.358, lines 143–150.
17. See pp.50–52.
18. Cf. I Kings 22.19 ff. where a 'spirit' offers to become a lying spirit in the mouth of the prophets to lure the king to his doom. This may serve to safeguard a doctrine of inspiration, but at the expense of raising serious questions about the character of God.
19. Two other examples spring to mind – Isaiah 45.15 where the translators could not accept that God could be both 'hidden' and 'a saviour', and Ecclesiastes 7.12 where the NEB translates 'Better have wisdom behind you than money' whereas Koheleth is in fact advocating both wisdom and wealth.
20. Daiches, op. cit., p.2.
21. See pp.62–64.
22. Among the Psalms reflecting such an attitude are Psalms 1, 3, 7, 10, 11, 17, 26, 28, 32, 36, 37, 50, 75, 91, 92, 96, 97, 112.
23. M. Buber, 'The Heart Determines' in *Theodicy in the Old Testament*, p.113.
24. For an interesting discussion of Jesus ben Sirach's contribution see J. L. Crenshaw in *Theodicy in the Old Testament*, pp.119–140.
25. Buber, op. cit., p.113.
26. Eichrodt in *Theodicy in the Old Testament*, p.36.

6. The Problem of Death

1. Cf. A. Leo Oppenheimer's wise words of warning about the dangers of generalizing concerning Mesopotamian religion in *Ancient Mesopotamia*, Chicago 1964, chapter 10.

2. J. Cerny (ed)., *Ancient Egyptian Religion*, Westport 1979, p.79. For a discussion of Egyptian concepts and terminology relating to survival after death see H. Frankfort, *Ancient Egyptian Religion: an Interpretation*, New York 1961, p.89.

3. Frankfort, op. cit., p.89.

4. Ibid., p.109.

5. *ANET*, pp.33–34.

6. Cf. W. McKane, *Proverbs*.

7. Oppenheimer, op. cit., p.176.

8. S. N. Kramer, *The Sumerians: their history, culture and character*, Chicago 1963, p.129.

9. Ibid., p.135.

10. W. G. Lambert, *Babylonian Wisdom Literature*, p.101.

11. *ANET*, p.102.

12. Translation W. G. Lambert, op. cit., p.12.

13. Translation H. W. F. Saggs, *The Greatness that was Babylon*, London 1962, p.404.

14. *ANET*, p.96.

15. I agree with McKane that it is not necessary to see in this foreign woman a foreign cultic official. Rather it is a woman of loose morals regarded as a dangerous outsider by society.

16. In this respect Sheol may be modelled on *Mot* the god of death in Ugaritic mythology.

17. See R. Gordis, *Koheleth, the Man and his World*, New York 1968, ad. loc.

18. Cf. Gordis, op. cit.; J. L. Crenshaw, *Ecclesiastes* (Old Testament Library Series) London 1988; J. Sawyer, 'The Ruined House in Ecclesiastes 12. A Reconstruction of the Original Parable', *JBL*, 94 (1976), pp.519–533.

19. A. R. Johnson, *The Vitality of the Individual in the Thought of Ancient Israel*, Cardiff 1964, p.85.

20. L. G. Perdue, *Wisdom and Cult*, p.318.

21. E. Gerstenberger, op. cit., p.206; but again his arguments for locating the Psalm in the post-exilic age seem to me far from convincing.

22. The textual detail in this verse is extremely difficult, but the general meaning is hardly in doubt.

23. E.g. A. Weiser, *Psalms* (Old Testament Library Series), London and Philadelphia 1962, ad. loc.; A. A. Anderson, *Psalms*, ad loc.

24. M. Dahood, *Psalms II*, ad loc.

25. Cf. pp.70f.

26. J. Calvin, *Commentary on the Book of Psalms*, Edinburgh 1845–49, ad loc.

27. The almost insoluble translation problems in this verse can be seen not only in the RSV footnotes, but by comparing the RSV with the NEB and with Habel's translation.

28. For a view radically at odds with this see Dahood, *Psalms*. His arguments, heavily dependent upon what are claimed to be Ugaritic parallels, are far from convincing.

7. Wisdom and Worship – The Contribution of Jesus ben Sirach

1. I. Levi, *The Hebrew Text of the Book of Ecclesiasticus*, Leiden 1904, reprint ed. R. Gottheil, M. Jastrow, 1969. M. H. Segal, *Seper ben Sira ha salem*, Jerusalem 1958.

2. For a discussion of the extent to which creation material, Genesis 1–11 and Second Isaiah shape Ben Sirach's thought see an unpublished thesis by K. Burton, *Sirach and the Judaic Doctrine of Creation*, University of Glasgow 1987.

3. A. Schokel in *Israelite Wisdom*, p.242.

4. I. Levi, op. cit. p.78.

5. I owe this useful expression to W. D. Davies.

6. R. Gordis, *Koheleth, the Man and His World*, New York 1969 ad loc.

7. See pp.27–30.

8. See pp.71f.

9. See pp.70–72.

10. *Theodicy in the Old Testament*, p.120.

11. J. L. Crenshaw, *Theodicy in the Old Testament*, p.130.

12. See pp.90–91.

8. Songs of God's People – Then and Now

1. This is true even for Jesus ben Sirach, unless like B. S. Childs we restrict the Old Testament canon to the Hebrew, a verdict for which there is little justification in Christian tradition; see B. S. Childs, *An Introduction to the Old Testament as Scripture*, London and Philadelphia 1979.

2. J. A. Sanders, *Torah and Canon*, Philadelphia 1972, p.xiv.

3. See the discussion of such issues in D. Nineham, *The Use and Abuse of the Bible*, London 1976; J. Barr, *Holy Scripture: Canon, Authority, Criticism*, Oxford 1983; E. Best, *From Text to Sermon*, Edinburgh 1978.

4. *God and the Poets*, pp.88–111.

5. If with the NEB we read the last line 'and their prayers are about their daily work', it gives a different perspective but hardly alters the point I wish to make.

6. *Songs of God's People*, Oxford 1988.

7. *Songs of God's People* 21, from the songbook 'Love from Below', copyright 1989 Iona Community, Wild Goose Publications, Pearce Institute, Govan, Glasgow G51 3UT, used by permission.

8. Ian Fraser, *Songs of God's People* 80, quoted with the permission of the publishers Stainer and Bell Ltd, London and Galaxy Music, Boston Mass. copyright Stainer and Bell Ltd 1969.

9. *Be Our Freedom Lord*, Lutheran Publication House, Adelaide 1981. Quotations are made with kind permission of Terry Falla.

10. Ibid., p.149.

11. J. Habgood, *Confessions of a Conservative Liberal*, London 1988, p.94.

12. G. von Rad, *Wisdom in Israel*, London 1971, p.107.

13. See pp.47–64.

14. Habgood, op. cit. p.206.

15. Fred Pratt Green, *Songs of God's People* 116, quoted with the permission of the publishers Stainer and Bell Ltd, London and Hope Publishing Co., Carol Stream, IL 60188, USA, copyright 1971, all rights reserved.

16. D. F. Morgan, *Wisdom in the Old Testament Traditions*, Atlanta 1981.

17. See p.56.

18. Habgood, op. cit., p.95.

Index of References

OLD TESTAMENT

APOCRYPHA

Index of Names

(References to the notes are omitted where these coincide with a text
reference.)